P9-BYJ-572

BUSINESS, SCIENCE & TECHNOLOGY DEPT.
BIRMINGHAM PUBLIC LIBRARY
2100 PARK PLACE
BIRMINGHAM, ALABAMA 35203

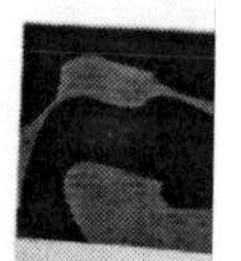

Guerrilla STREET TEAM Guide

Helping Teamers and Business People Alike Utilize Guerrilla Marketing Strategies on the Grassroots Level to Reach People Not Typically Exposed to Traditional Advertising

Jay Conrad Levinson
& Brad Lovejoy

Guerrilla Street Team Guide

By Jay Conrad Levinson & Brad Lovejoy

© 2008 All rights reserved.

No part of this publication may be reproduced or transmitted in any form or by any means, mechanical or electronic, including photocopying and recording, or by any information storage and retrieval system, without permission in writing from author or publisher (except by a reviewer, who may quote brief passages and/or show brief video clips in a review).

ISBN: 978-1-60037-392-3 (Paperback)
LCCN: 2008922720

Published by:

Morgan James Publishing, LLC
1225 Franklin Ave. Suite 325
Garden City, NY 11530-1693
800.485.4943
www.MorganJamesPublishing.com

Editing by:

Jon Elliston
Managing Editor of Mountain Xpress and author of Psywar on Cuba: The Declassified History of U.S. Anti-Castro Propaganda and co-author of North Carolina Curiosities: Quirky Characters, Roadside Oddities & Other Offbeat Stuff

Cover & Interior Designs by:

Megan Johnson
Johnson2Design
www.Johnson2Design.com
megan@Johnson2Design.com

Dedication

DEDICATION

To my loving wife Michelle, who has been most patient and encouraging from the beginning. To my parents and stepparents, thank you for teaching me to reach for my dreams while enjoying the here and now. To my extended family, I couldn't have made it without you. Thanks to each music industry professional that shared their insight and time. To Greg Bogard, Chuck Kerzac and Dr. Pascal Young for teaching me to read between the lines of music. To Larry Groce, the host of Mountain Stage, who graciously took the time to help me chart my course in the music industry. Thanks to Morgan James Publishing, it has been a real pleasure. To every group that hopes to make their dreams come true—this book is for you!

– BL

Table of Contents

TABLE OF CONTENTS

Introduction

INTRODUCTION

This book is designed as a handbook. It will not tell you every last detail about Guerrilla Marketing, nor will it go into great depth about the music industry. What it will do, however, is give you a complete picture of how Guerrilla Street Team Marketing works. You will know enough by the end of this book to be able to create and manage your own street team. Even if you are not directly responsible for the management of a street team, a greater understanding of how street teams fit in to the marketing picture will help you communicate better with those who do such work. Each chapter builds on and works off the preceding ones. At the end of each chapter, you will find an exercise and action steps to help you focus on your project. At the end of the book, you will find some additional information—from some of the music industry's most respected professionals—about street team marketing.

CHAPTER 1:
What is Guerrilla Street Team Marketing?

Guerilla Street Team Marketing is a combination of traditional event promotion and viral, peer-to-peer and live marketing that employs teams of supporters who use philosophies of Guerrilla Marketing on the grassroots level.

– B. Lovejoy

I'm assuming many of those reading these words are involved in and knowledgeable about the ever-evolving music industry, some are aspiring to be and many have a product or service they'd like to promote by using street teams. Maybe you're a student with no prior knowledge about street teams, or you're simply curious about street team marketing. Maybe you're a senior manager who wants to learn more. Or you could be the band's biggest fan and now manage the street team. In this book, we talk about bands and your role as a manager, promoter, label executive or intern. If you're reading because you're involved with a different project, change the examples to meet your needs.

This Guerrilla Street Team Marketing course will cover 17 Guerrilla Marketing concepts that guarantee success, the 200 Guerilla Marketing weapons, the structure for a seven-step Guerrilla Street Team Marketing strategy and the 10 steps you must take to succeed in the music industry!

Along with these concepts, the course will provide additional Internet links that you will need to apply your knowledge in the real world. Whether you're interested in increasing your band's, venue's or event's profits, or simply curious about where to begin, keep reading! I give you valuable information that can greatly increase the success of any project. This book is an opportunity to share my knowledge and a chance to give something back to the music community and the world. So, without any further ado, here are the basics of Guerrilla Street Team Marketing…

WHAT IS MARKETING IN THE FIRST PLACE?

For veteran guerrillas, this will be a refresher.

Marketing is the sum of all contact your band or company has with the public (buying, selling and advertising). Guerrillas view marketing as a circle that starts with your income-generating idea and extends to repeat and referral customers. In this book, fans and customers are the same thing. Instead of calling them repeat customers, let's call them dedicated fans.

These dedicated fans are the heart and soul of the music industry and it is important to treat them like friends.

When fans tell other people how much they liked the show or event, when people can't get enough encores and are dying to hear one more song ... that's the kind of marketing we're after! Webster's dictionary defines marketing as "all business activity involved in the moving of goods from the producer to the consumer, including selling, advertising, packaging, etc."

WHAT IS A STREET TEAM?

A street team is comprised of dedicated fans that hit the streets to inform the public about a band, festival, venue, product or service. Before every show, street team members, often referred to as street teamers, are hanging up posters, passing out fliers and other promotional items, promoting online and talking to people they meet on the street, urging them to go to an event, try a sample or otherwise consume a product. Strategic flier distribution and Guerilla Street Team Marketing reaches an audience that doesn't access advertising via TV, magazines or radio.

Most street team members volunteer their time in exchange for free event tickets and merchandise. In addition to promoting, they provide much-needed information and feedback about new markets and help establish a fan base. Dedicated fans are what push a band or event to the top.

From the clay tablets of Babylon to the papyri of the ancient Egyptians, people have been getting the word out about news, events, products and services for a long time. The Greeks used town criers to announce the arrival of ships carrying trade goods. Then, all of Europe started using them.

In the 1980s, major record labels noticed what was going on in the punk scene, as well as, what was happening on the streets of Hollywood, and started using street teams on a national level. Punk and independent bands were using street teams to promote their upcoming shows and albums. These typically unpaid teams were often teenagers and college students who were rewarded with free band merchandise or show access in exchange for spreading the word.

VH1 highlighted this in their special feature "When Metal Ruled the World." Bands playing in the same neighborhoods would compete for public advertising space by ripping each other's fliers down and replacing them with their own. This became known as "The Flier Wars."

In the 1990s, before street teaming wasn't a common term but was a common practice, record labels called their street team members representatives or "reps." From the era of the town crier to time of the paperboy, from the record label representative to the street team member, peer-to-peer marketing has always worked, and it always will.

The passion of your fan base can be the most effective and inexpensive means of promoting your band. Do everything you can to capitalize on the grassroots buzz that is already out there happening. Peer-to-peer communication is far more powerful than standard print/internet advertising and should be utilized as such.

–Matt Hogan, Marketing Director of SCI Fidelity Records/Madison House Presents

HOW IS GUERRILLA STREET TEAM MARKETING DIFFERENT FROM TRADITIONAL STREET TEAM MARKETING?

Guerrilla Marketing is unconventional, not-by-the-book, and extremely flexible. Guerrilla Marketing does not mean illegal marketing; it teaches us to cooperate with our competitors and the cities in which we do business. Most of all, Guerrilla Marketing is a way for business owners to spend less, get more, and achieve substantial profits.

–Jay Conrad Levinson

On January 31, 2007, several magnetic light displays in and around the city of Boston were mistaken for possible explosive devices. The displays were intended to help a TV program gain exposure. Later, city and state officials came to an agreement with Turner Broadcasting Systems and Interference Inc. to pay for costs incurred during the incident. As part of a settlement that resolves all criminal and civil claims, they agreed to pay $2 million. $1 million of this went towards the Boston police department, and $1 million went towards homeland security. In addition, a statement was released to take responsibility and apologize for the incident. Don't break any laws. Do your homework. Brainstorm about possible negative outcomes and always be considerate of others!

On a different but similar note, some street teams hang posters in illegal places, cover up other people's posters or rip them down. It is also illegal to place fliers in or magnets on newspaper boxes. These kinds of behaviors may be referred to as "hostile guerrilla activities." Many major record labels and music promotion companies already have street teams, but they are not operating under the Guerrilla Marketing philosophy. Guerrilla Street Team Marketing shares the ground-level philosophy behind Guerrilla Marketing.

Twenty factors make Guerilla Marketing different from conventional marketing:

1. Instead of investing money in the marketing process, we invest time, energy,

information and IMAGINATION. For example, does your street team promotional package come with a thank you note? Get crazy. Think outside the box's box!

Sample Thank You Note:

Thank You!

(Your band's name) and (concert promoter) would like to thank you for your energy and support. Helping us spread the word about (your band's name) makes all the difference in the world. We want you to know how much we appreciate your help!

Street teaming is more than being just a fan - it's spreading the word to friends and music fans, and of course handing out lots of fliers! Your efforts help us to bring you a bigger and better (event or tour name) every year. We are truly thankful for all of your effort.

Thank you for supporting (your band's name) and live music! We'll see you on (date)!

– Your Band

www.yourband.com

2. Instead of gambling with marketing dollars, we use market research, the sciences of psychology and sociology, and understanding of human behavior.

3. Profits, press coverage and event attendance are the main indicators by which we measure the success of our marketing.

4. Guerrilla Marketing, similar to grassroots marketing, was created to suit small business however—it can now be applied to large-scale promotions and operations.

5. Instead of dismissing fans and street team members once they've helped us, we are obligated to follow-up. Follow a sale or newsletter sign-up with a gift and survey to solicit ideas and feedback. After a concert, e-mail, call or send an after-show promotional package to reward each street team member.

6. Guerrilla Marketing removes the mystery from the marketing process by creating strategies, plans, calendars and budgets.

7. Instead of focusing on competition, Guerrilla Marketing encourages coopera-

tion, urging us to help each other. No guerrilla left behind!

8. Instead of merely trying to push their bands, guerrillas build strong relationships and consequently generate more than just one sale.

9. Instead of relying on a single marketing weapon, guerrillas know that only marketing *combinations* work and that marketing is the sum of all contact with the public.

10. Guerrilla philosophy teaches us that advertising is only one of many marketing weapons.

11. Instead of growing too quickly, guerrillas grow profitably and maintain their focus. For example, a band should successfully complete a regional tour before booking a national or international tour.

12. Instead of targeting the masses, Guerrilla Marketing aims for individuals and small groups.

13. Guerrilla Marketing is always intentional and embraces such details as how the

telephone is answered or the paper on which the thank you note is printed.

14. Instead of growing linearly by adding new customers, guerrillas grow geometrically by increasing the size and meaning of each transaction, generating repeat sales, leaning upon the referral power of customers, and then adding new customers. The Grateful Dead are a perfect example of this approach. Many of their dedicated fans traveled with them from show to show for many and bought millions in merchandise. Their fame grew to global proportions without relying on conventional marketing.

15. Guerrilla Marketing asks that we think of what a business can give in the way of free information and useful promotional products and services to help customers and prospects.

16. Instead of being fearful of the digital revolution, Guerrilla Marketing encourages us to embrace the latest technological changes and stay up to date.

17. Guerrilla Marketing is all about direct communication between a business and a targeted consumer.

18. Instead of focusing on sales, Guerrilla Marketing attempts to gain consent with marketing, then uses that consent to effectively market ONLY to interested people.

19. Instead of being a monolog, Guerrilla Marketing is an interactive dialog. The Internet is an ideal platform for this exchange to occur.

20. By mobilizing street teams, we interact with prospects on the street or on the web one-on-one and build strong relationships, brand recognition and loyalty.

These are very important distinctions and allow the concept of Guerrilla Marketing to fill a void in the world economy. It is no surprise that Guerrilla Marketing books have been translated into 43 languages, sold more than 15 million copies, are required reading in most MBA programs, are available in audio and videotape versions, as computer software, a nationally-syndicated column, a newsletter, and an interactive association, and are the most popular and widely-read marketing books in the world.

> *In order to manage a successful street team program, it is essential that the street team coordinator be in constant communication with his or her team.*
>
> –Tom Russell, National Promotions Director of Superfly Productions

GUERRILLA EXERCISE:

See if your existing strategies are aligned with the 20 facets of Guerrilla Marketing. The goal is to run your campaign with all 20 factors in mind.

Put a checkmark next to each factor you're already putting into action. Furthermore, brainstorm how you *are* or *could* employ each factor.

❒ I invest time, energy and **imagination** rather than only money.

❒ My marketing is based on research rather than optimism.

❒ I measure my marketing performance by profits and fan base.

❒ I embrace the principles of small business marketing more than large business marketing.

❒ I follow-up all shows, street team campaigns

and sales with customer contact and never ignore the fans or street team members.

- ❒ I feel in control and am not afraid of the marketing process.
- ❒ I'm creating allies and co-marketing programs with them.
- ❒ I update my address book monthly.
- ❒ I use combinations of marketing weapons rather than relying on one.
- ❒ I utilize an assortment of marketing tools in the attainment of my business goals.
- ❒ I focus my energy on established fans rather than looking for new prospects.
- ❒ I carefully plan each step of my company's marketing; I know marketing is any contact between my company and anyone else.
- ❒ I direct my marketing to individuals and small groups.
- ❒ I strive to grow at a controlled rate.
- ❒ I freely give things away that can help my customers and prospects attain their own goals.

- ❐ I use technology to strengthen my marketing and I have no fear of using it.

- ❐ My marketing messages are stated very directly—from my prospects' and customers' points of view rather than my own.

- ❐ My marketing gains consent from people to receive my marketing materials.

- ❐ I make my marketing a dialog and always request feedback.

- ❐ I use street teams to reach my target audience and to provide feedback.

GUERRILLA ACTION STEPS:

A. Note the numbers at which no checkmark appears. These are the areas that you need altering in your method of marketing.

B. Decide upon the specific actions that you will take for each statement. Polish and perfect your marketing by transforming it to embrace the philosophies of Guerrilla Marketing. List these ideas for improvement in the space provided beneath each statement.

C. Turn your new ideas into actions, one by one, until each of the statements deserves a checkmark.

CHAPTER 2:
The Mechanics Of
Guerrilla Street
Team Marketing

THE MECHANICS OF A STREET TEAM

People are much more likely to follow through for someone they've met personally (and might even consider a friend) versus a nameless and faceless entity.

–Matt Hogan, Marketing Director of SCI Fidelity Records/Madison House Presents

Each national or regional street team has a manager or coordinator. This person develops grassroots and stunt marketing efforts and incentive programs, builds weekly and monthly calendars to ensure proper staffing of each event, recruits and street team members, oversees accounting and shipping of all promotional items, evaluates team member reports and awards compensation, creates and sends newsletters, and nurtures effective leaders into area captains. For the street team manager, life will be an endless weekly cycle of recruiting and following up with team members. Each show has a simple routine: create a plan, launch the attack and evaluate the results.

I think it is great to go out with the teams, if possible, and show them that you are not afraid to sweat and be a part of the team. It's not just sitting at a desk and sending out packages!

–Jay Nadolny, Systems Account Coordinator of GMR Marketing

WHO ARE WE RECRUITING AND FOR WHAT?

When we are recruiting prospects to join the street team, we never stop until we've reached our goals.

The important thing about direct marketing is that it seeks a response. It involves the planned recording, analysis and tracking of individual customers' responses and transactions for the purpose of developing and prolonging profitable customer relationships.

It is crucial to have prospects' permission before wasting your time and money trying to market to them! People that sign up for newsletters are giving you permission to market to them. Do it well, entertain them, give them what they want and you will succeed.

Money Saving Tips:

- Keep your labor costs down by setting goals so that you don't waste time over-recruiting
- Save money by only marketing to people who have given you their permission

RECRUITING ONLINE

There are several methods for recruiting online, such as posting on forums, social networking sites and message boards, using existing mass e-mailing lists and sending individual e-mails and e-cards. You can reduce your workload by delegating the task of recruiting to street team members.

- Research the forum culture by observing before initiating conversations or posting your information
- Don't waste the group's time by simply agreeing or spamming
- Be helpful to gain respect
- Use your company signature
- Check the board frequently
- BE PATIENT!

HOW TO GET THE SAME RESULTS AS THE MAJORS

Major record labels understand the value of street teams and every successful band has a street team. Music industry professionals and independent bands know the importance of street team marketing; being a street team manager for a successful band is a full-time job. Many bands augment their radio and online promotions by asking their street team members to repeatedly call radio stations and ask for the band's music to be played. It is common practice to create multiple online profiles and e-mail addresses for the purpose of producing a false fan base, thus making the band look successful in the eyes of an out-of-town talent buyer. In this book, we're focused on getting people to tell their friends about something they believe in and support.

The first thing you need to do is decide who you look up to. Then, read their newsletters and decide what you liked about them. Write down everything from formatting to fonts to colors. Then, research other bands in their genre; their competitors. Decide what you like about their approaches and write it down. Don't waste your time writing down things you don't like. Reading different newsletters and invitations, you will quickly notice that format, grammar and writing styles change dramatically across the industry spectrum.

Write to Your Target Audience:

- Visualize it, set a goal and work toward it
- Write different newsletters for different subgroups
- Keep a journal of ideas that you like about your competitors' marketing

To save time, create, cut and paste street team invitation and newsletter templates and subject lines. Open a window for both the body and subject. Highlight both selections. You can use the keyboard functions, like cut and paste, with your left hand while using the mouse with your right. This is especially useful for sending peer-to-peer messages on social networking sites such as MySpace.

7 things to remember about sending street team invitations:

1. Choose an appealing e-mail address and subject line (i.e. streetteam@yourband.com; Want FREE Tickets?)

2. Customize street team invitations and newsletters for different subgroups (i.e. creating gender or age specific invitations for social networking sites that allow you to sort by gender or age)

3. Keep it short

4. Check the formatting before sending invitations or newsletters - send a test message to yourself—because typos devastate your reputation and professional image

5. Provide information, not hype

6. Stay on the topic

7. Ask for four points of contact initially in the invitation: first and last names, mailing address, phone number and e-mail address. Sometimes, a respondent will only their provide nickname with their mailing address. Clearly ask for all four points of contact in your initial street team invitation to save time and decrease labor costs.

Sample Thank You Note:

Sample Street Team Invitation:

(Your band's name with a hyperlink to its website) is coming to your town and we're looking for a few energetic people to join our street team! (Your band's name) is playing at (venue's name with a hyperlink to its website) on (date)!

We need street team members to help us spread the word by passing out fliers and re-posting this message all over the Internet! If you'd like to pass out fliers and generally spread the word, we'd like to thank you with a spot on the guest list and some stickers!

It's sooo easy to spread the word:

-before the bar, @ the bar, @ the after-party!

-meet new people, little commitment, lots of fun!

-build your music industry resume; support the local scene, GET ON THE GUEST LIST!

Just e-mail me with your first and last name, mailing address and phone number. We would really love the help!

I'll look forward to hearing from you,

-(your name)
Street Team Manager
(your company's website)

Where: (Venue's Name)

(venue's website with hyperlink)

(venue's physical address)

(venue's phone number)

*Note use of bold font

RECRUITING AND PROMOTING AT THE SHOW

After you have researched your competition and targeted their fans, the rest is up to you and your street team. The act of street teaming is basically passing out stickers and bottle openers, right? Wrong, think of it as distributing collectible memorabilia. It is important to choose promotional materials and Guerrilla Street Team Marketing scripts that are right for your target audiences.

For example, if the band you are promoting is a wild group, you wouldn't want conservative street team members—you'd want the wildest people you could find to distribute promotional items. Carefully select your candidates that will represent you at shows. In the corporate sector, paid street team members, who often staff in-store promotions or special events, are referred to as promotional models.

Portable media such as iPods, LCD backpacks and personal digital assistants (PDAs) are changing the landscape of street team and live marketing. Street team members can now present a multimedia experience by simply pressing play.

THE PEN VERSUS THE PDA

When recruiting new street team members or newsletter sign-ups at shows, it is important to be fast and accurate. Let's compare the traditional method of recruiting by attaching a pen to a clipboard and leaving it on the merchandise table to a street team member using a PDA.

PDA pros:

- Easy for the prospect because they do not have to enter any information
- No manual data transfer after show, thus reducing labor costs and risk of errors
- No typos
- Visible in low light
- Holds massive amounts of data

PDA cons:

- Device may fail
- Expensive
- Sensitive to weather conditions

Pen pros:

- Allows you to design attractive sign-up sheets
- Is cheaper
- Takes very little training or explanation to be effective

Pen cons:

- Does not work well in low light
- Sensitive to weather conditions
- Manual data transfer is time consuming and increases the rise of error

Each major market should have an area captain. This person is ideally the best of the best in street team marketing! They're organized, cool, resourceful and reliable. Often, area captains are dedicated fans who are personally connected to the band. Some street team managers prefer to send one large package of promotional items to area captains and have them personally distribute its contents to other street team members. This builds community and removes the anonymity of the street team member, thus making them feel more personally accountable. However, it may be inconvenient for some street team members to meet up with area captains. I prefer sending individual packages, making distribution as convenient as possible for each street team member.

I recommend using at least eight street team members per city. Working in pairs will make being on the street safer, easier and more fun. Assign each pair or team a section of town: north, south, east and west. For nationally advertised events and promotions, like large festivals, at least

100 street team members are necessary. Smaller bands tend to resist using larger street teams because they want to keep their guest list numbers down. However, they aren't seeing the big picture; they aren't thinking long term. They don't see that using as many interested street team members as possible engages and grows their fan base. Guerrilla Marketing teaches us to think long term.

BOOST YOUR ALBUM AND TICKET SALES BY HOSTING A LISTENING OR VIEWING PARTY!

Many bands and labels are now including 'listening parties' in their advertising budget. A listening or viewing party is a house party, at which a CD or DVD is played or shown. Area captains are especially good for hosting listening parties and other events. The sponsor provides the catering, listening materials and other supplies. The area captains are responsible for the venue, logistical coordination and advertising. Parties like these provide a great opportunity for surprise artist appearances or an organized "meet-n-greet" with an autograph session, behind the scenes video footage, etc.

Experiences like these have a huge impact on fans. This type of personal connection builds long-term brand loyalty. It's gaining fans, one by one, day by day. It's real and the fans know it. Most bands cringe at the term brand loyalty, brand loyalty means a fan chooses to see your show again, instead of another band at the venue next door.

Scheduling times for everyone to get together when we are not working lets people get to know each other and makes it more fun at upcoming shows. Putting things on a personal level inspires people to help more.

– Lisa Cyr, Street Team Coordinator of AC Entertainment

Recruit prospects that are street-smart or streetwise to pass out fliers and hang posters. This means that they are knowledgeable about environments where vice and crime are prevalent. Every person who wants to help has a specialty and it is the street team manager's job to find out what that is and assign appropriate tasks.

It is important to choose the right kind of street team member for each task. There are different areas of street teaming: talking to people at shows or on the street and passing out fliers, talking to people on the phone, promoting online and distributing posters. A good manager understands each member's personality and assigns appropriate tasks. For example, the most extroverted and outgoing people should pass stuff out at concerts, festivals and on the street. These people love handing stuff out and talking to people. Introverted people typically gravitate towards promoting online and putting up posters because it doesn't involve direct communication with the public. By maintaining a close relationship with each of your street team members, you'll know who is introverted and who is extroverted.

It is also important to properly train each member. Assume each new member knows nothing about a street team or marketing. Basics like how to properly tape a poster, hand out a flier and handle rejection from people who won't take a flier should be included in the introductory information. Write down what your street team members need to say – this is known as a script. Practicing scripts lead to increased self-confidence.

> *Leadership is the key component in managing a street team effectively. Good leaders execute great campaigns.*
>
> – James M. Aquafredda, National Managing Director of Street Team Promotion

Each street team member needs a pack and poster tube. The pack holds all necessary street teaming supplies: small notebook, pen, marker, tape, tacks, rubber mallet for tapping thumb tacks into wood, pliers for removing old staples and tacks, waste container for old staples and tacks, digital camera, water, cell phone, small flashlight, iPod, and handbills. I prefer to use a lumbar pack because it's easier to take on the bus and holds all the necessary items. Poster tubes are helpful when dealing with several large posters. Many street team members ride the bus or walk around town; having a pack and poster tube makes the whole process much easier and protects your items from the elements.

Organizational Tips:

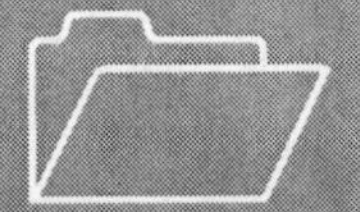

- Make sure to place a rubber band around your posters before putting them in the poster tube
- Keep a waterproof container or bag inside your pack to protect your electronics and handbills in the rain and snow

Being a good street team manager means understanding each street team member's motivation and personality type. Some will join the street team for free tickets or to make new friends. Other team members will be building their resumes. Retain team members by giving them what they want. Managing an effective street team means understanding positive reinforcement. Street team members of different ages and backgrounds will need to be motivated differently. You have to have good incentives to get people to spend their time and energy helping you. Try to determine why each member joined and compensate each member accordingly.

Motivational Tips:

- Use satin or laminated VIP passes to reward effective street team members
- Sell surplus passes as memorabilia after the tour

Any time you can go above and beyond and give them something you can't put a price tag on—a signed CD or poster, a VIP or after-show pass, a chance to meet their favorite musician face-to-face—you're going to get a much better response, and you'll have a far greater follow-through and loyalty from your street team.

– Matt Hogan, Marketing Director of SCI Fidelity Records/Madison House Presents

Poster Distribution Tip:

- Distributing posters at night or in the early morning is easier because there is less traffic
- Vehicles that make frequent stops or park in loading zones should be identified as a delivery vehicle. Caution lights are relatively cheap, available at any auto parts store and could save the team member a parking ticket—or prevent an accident.

A good street team manager thinks about the safety and comfort of their street team members. In windy conditions, it is much easier and faster to put up a poster if you have help. A street team manager can transform a bunch of strangers into friends. **The primary goal of the street team manager is to build community and to inspire fans to promote their favorite band, event, venue, service or product.**

TIMELINES

For large national and international festivals and events, start recruiting at least a year in advance and mail promotional materials no later than six months prior to the event.

For smaller local events:

- Recruit four to six weeks before show
- Mail materials at least two weeks before show
- Follow up with street team members and newsletter subscribers within a week of the show

Make sure to include in the after-show promotional package:

- Thank you note
- Incentive or reward
- Survey (about show, venue, merchandise, etc.)

REPORTING

Street team managers are expected to give their clients progress reports. Jot down accomplishments and compile a daily report. Then, outline weekly activities to your client on a monthly basis; include photos and an expenditure report.

Simple Monthly Report:

This month we sent two newsletters, 2,000 street team invitations via MySpace and other social networking sites, received 25 photo reports and mailed 67 promotional packages to five major markets (NYC, Austin, Chicago, L.A., Nashville); 70 hours of labor, total expenditure: $1735.

THE PATH OF THE GUERRILLA

As marketing continues to change, the secrets of Guerrilla Marketing continue to change. Originally, there were three secrets, then seven, then 12 then 16. Here are the 17 secrets that guarantee you will succeed:

1. **COMMITMENT:** A mediocre marketing program with commitment will always prove more profitable than a brilliant marketing program without commitment. Commitment makes it happen.

2. **INVESTMENT:** Marketing is not an expense, but an investment—the best investment available, if you do it correctly.

3. **CONSISTENT:** It takes a while for music fans to trust you, and if you change your marketing, media and identity, you're hard to trust. Restraint is a great ally of the guerrilla. Repetition is another.

4. **CONFIDENT:** Being confident is a major factor in succeeding. Know what your goals are and be prepared. Your clients and street team members need to feel like you have things under control—so be in control and you will be confident.

5. **PATIENT:** Unless the person running your marketing is patient, it will be difficult to practice commitment, view marketing as an investment, be consistent and make prospects confident. Patience is a guerrilla virtue.

6. **ASSORTMENT:** Guerrillas know that individual marketing weapons rarely work on their own. But marketing combinations do work. A wide assortment of marketing tools is required to woo and win customers.

7. **CONVENIENT:** People now know that time is more valuable than money. Respect this by running your operation for the convenience of your clients, not yourself.

8. **AMAZEMENT:** There are elements of your show that you take for granted, but the prospects would be amazed if they knew the details. Be sure your marketing always reflects that amazement.

9. **SUBSEQUENT:** The real profits come after you've made the sale, in the form of repeat and referral business. Non-guerrillas think marketing ends when they've made the sale. Guerrillas know that is when true marketing begins.

10. **MEASUREMENT:** Unless you measure the effectiveness of each weapon, you won't know which weapon is hitting the bull's-eye.

11. **INVOLVEMENT:** This describes the relationship between you and your customers - and it is a relationship. You prove your involvement by following up; they prove theirs by patronizing and recommending you.

12. **DEPENDENT:** The guerrilla's job is not to compete but to cooperate with other businesses. Market them in return for them marketing you. Set up tie-ins with others. Become dependent on your allies to market more and invest less.

13. **ARMAMENT:** Armament is defined as "the equipment necessary to wage and win battles." The armament of Guerrilla Street Team Marketers is technology, fliers, posters, stickers, tape, tacks and the ability to positively interact on a grassroots level.

14. **CONSENT:** In an era of non-stop interruption marketing, the key to success is to first gain consent to receive your marketing materials, then market to only to those who have given you that consent. Don't waste money on people who don't give you their permission to market to them!

15. **AUGMENT:** To succeed online, augment your website with offline promotion, constant maintenance of your site, participation in newsgroups and forums, e-mail, chat room attendance, posting articles, hosting conferences and rapid follow-up.

16. **CONTENT:** Marketing is information that can benefit the lives of those to whom it is aimed. Marketing must make the truth fascinating. For marketing to live up to that definition, it has to be rich in content.

17. **ENTERTAINMENT:** People love to be entertained. From fireside stories to street performances, give them what they want and they will keep coming back for more!

DATA COLLECTION: THE MODERN WHEEL

> *Find out everything about your target audience, and then get your information into their hands.*
>
> – Danny Ornelas, National Director of Marketing of MySpace Records

One of the greatest challenges a street team manager will face is organizing team members' information such as name, mailing address, telephone number and e-mail address—as well as their progress reports.

In the past, simple spreadsheets were used to compile street team members' contact information. Each major market and state was designated a folder to store the street team members' data. This process of manual categorization is very labor intensive. Today, databases have been designed specifically to meet the needs of today's street team. If you can't afford a modern database, manual categorization still works and is the place for bands and festivals on a limited budget to start.

The new interactive web-based Fancorps (www.Fancorps.com) system relies on an incredibly detailed Web 2.0 based application that combines the best of database management with MySpace-inspired interactive social networking. It uses a point and ranking system to give team members an incentive to do anything from posting comments and fliers around the Internet, to going to stores and putting up posters, to calling radio stations and requesting airplay of a single. Tasks are created and assigned by team leaders, and members of the band's team login and have the option to take on and complete those selected tasks and then be rewarded for them. The site also encompasses an impressive database or "intel" section that includes traditional retail stores and college/commercial radio stations, along with more "lifestyle locations" such as tattoo shops, coffee shops, clubs and anywhere else you could think of to promote a band or musician.

One of the most important things about managing a street team is to personally know who is on your team.

- Seth Weiner, Founder of Shimon Presents, Inc.

Dropcards, Inc., (www.dropcards.com), digital promotion company, has launched a nationwide online service for musicians to manage their own promotional efforts by using Dropcards' PIN-based download cards to bridge the gap between offline and online promotions and sales. Dropcards are the newest, coolest and most cost effective way to get your music and content out to new fans and quantify promotional performance. The card itself is a highly collectible, quality full-color plastic card that gives users exclusive access to your music and other content.

Before handing out free tickets to every applicant on the planet, you need to individually evaluate each street team member's performance. There are several methods of keeping track of the members' activity, ranging from old school to high tech.

Here is an actual progress report from a street team member:

Yo, Anna Doe and I were out for about 4 hours last night. Dropped off flyers at ev-

ery conceivable spot, record stores, coffee shops, etc., and put up almost all of the posters we had. We hit West Philly, University City, South Philly, South Street, Olde City, Manayunk and Roxboro... if you know any of those areas. Took some pictures like you asked. If you're keeping inventory, between the 2 of us, we have 13 posters, maybe 100 flyers left which I'm taking with me at lunch to put up out in the Philly suburbs.

Cheers,

John Doe

IS IT TIME TO HIRE AN OUT-SOURCED MARKETING FIRM?

You will know it is time to bring in outside support if managing the street team is demanding more time, energy and experience than you can give.

HOW DO YOU CHOOSE A FIRM THAT IS RIGHT FOR YOU?

Research a band, company or event that is similar to yours in size and genre. Contact their management firm and talk to them about your situation. Talking with a firm's staff will give you information about the office culture and help you make an informed decision.

Tips on Choosing an Out-Sourced Marketing Firm:

- Call and ask for a current and past client list or portfolio
- Talk with previous clients and examine their successes and failures
- Look at educational background, location and age of business
- Look beyond the hype
- Take them out to lunch
- Ask yourself, "Would I give them the key to my house or passwords to my accounts?"

GUERRILLA EXERCISE:

Measure your own organization by how many of these concepts dictate your marketing. Compare them, one by one, with the way you currently run your marketing program. The idea is to operate with a commitment to all 17.

Put a checkmark next to each of the guerrilla principles that you understand and embrace to run the marketing of your business; take notes about how you use each principal, or brainstorm ways to do so.

- Commitment
- Investment
- Consistent
- Confident
- Patient
- Assortment
- Convenient
- Subsequent
- Amazement
- Measurement
- Involvement
- Dependent
- Armament
- Consent
- Augment
- Content
- Entertainment

GUERRILLA ACTION STEPS:

A. Review the checklist above and circle the words where no checkmark appears. These are the areas that need altering in your method of marketing.

B. Decide on the specific actions you will take for each concept so you can capitalize on each secret of Guerrilla Marketing. List these in the space provided beneath each of the 17 concepts.

C. Take the actions you have listed, one by one, until each of the concepts deserves a checkmark.

CHAPTER 3: Guerrilla Street Team Marketing Weapons

Ask the average band manager what marketing is and you'll be told that it is advertising. Guerrillas know that this is nonsense. Advertising is only one weapon of marketing. How many weapons are most business owners aware of? **Guerrillas are aware of a full 200 Guerrilla Marketing weapons and make use of at least 40 of them.** More than half of the weapons are free! Here are ALL 200 weapons.

Each weapon is equally important, and only a combination of them will ensure success. Your job is to do what you can to use as many weapons as possible. You may not be familiar with every concept below but don't worry—you can learn everything you need to know about Guerrilla Marketing by visiting us on the web at www.gmarketing.com.

THE 200 WEAPONS OF GUERRILLA MARKETING

MINI-MEDIA

1. Marketing Plan
2. Marketing Calendar
3. Identity

4. Business Cards
5. Stationary
6. Personal Letters
7. Telephone Marketing
8. Toll-Free Number
9. Vanity Phone Number
10. Yellow Pages
11. Postcards
12. Post Card Deck
13. Classified Ads
14. Per Order/Inquiry Advertising
15. Free Ads in Shoppers
16. Circulars
17. Community Bulletin Boards
18. Movie Ads
19. Outside Signs
20. Street Banners
21. Window Display
22. Inside Signs
23. Posters
24. Canvassing
25. Door Hangers
26. Elevator Pitch
27. Value Story
28. Backends

29. Letters of Recommendation
30. Attendance at Trade Show

MAXI-MEDIA

31. Advertising
32. Direct Mail
33. Newspaper Ads
34. Radio Spots
35. Magazine Ads
36. Billboards
37. Television Commercials

E-MEDIA

38. Computer
39. Printer/Fax Machine
40. Chat Rooms
41. Forums Boards
42. Internet Bulletin Boards
43. List-building
44. Personalized E-mail
45. E-mail Signature Marketing
46. Canned E-mail
47. Bulk E-mail
48. Audio/Video postcards
49. Domain Name

50. Web Site
51. Landing Page
52. Merchant Account
53. Shopping Cart
54. Auto-Responders
55. Search Engine Ranking
56. Electronic Brochures
57. RSS Feeds
58. Blogs
59. Podcasting
60. Publish Own E-zine
61. Ads in Other E-zines
62. Write E-books
63. Provide Content (i.e. other web sites)
64. Produce Webinars
65. Joint Ventures
66. Word-of-Mouse
67. Viral Marketing
68. E-Bay/Auction Sites
69. Click Analyzers
70. Pay Per Click Ads
71. Search Engine Keywords
72. Google Adwords
73. Sponsored Links
74. Reciprocal Link Exchange

75. Banner Exchanges

76. Web Conversion Rate

INFO-MEDIA

77. Knowledge of Your Market

78. Research Studies

79. Specific Customer Data

80. Case Studies

81. Sharing

82. Brochures

83. Catalog

84. Business Directory

85. Public Service Announcements

86. Newsletter

87. A Speech

88. Free Consultations

89. Free Demonstrations

90. Free Seminars

91. Publish Article

92. Publish Column

93. Author a Book

94. Publishing-on-Demand

95. Speaker at Clubs

96. Teleseminars

97. Infomercials

98. Constant Learning

HUMAN-MEDIA

99. Marketing Insight
100. Yourself
101. Your Employees and Reps
102. Designated Guerrilla
103. Employee Attire
104. Social Demeanor
105. Target Audiences
106. Your Own Circle of Influence
107. Contact Time with Customers
108. How you say Hello and Goodbye
109. Teaching Ability
110. Stories
111. Sales Training
112. Use of Downtime
113. Networking
114. Professional Title
115. Affiliate Marketing
116. Media Contacts
117. List Customers
118. Core Story: Solution to Problem
119. Create a Sense of Urgency
120. Offer Limited Items/Time

121. Call to Action
122. Satisfied Customers

NON-MEDIA

123. Benefits List
124. Competitive Advantages
125. Gifts
126. Service
127. Public Relations
128. Fusion Marketing
129. Barter
130. Word-of-Mouth
131. Buzz
132. Community Involvement
133. Club Memberships
134. Free Directory Listings
135. Trade Show Booth
136. Special Events
137. Name Tags at Events
138. Luxury Box at Events
139. Gift Certificates
140. Audio/Visual Aids
141. Flipcharts
142. Reprints and Blowups
143. Coupons

144. Free Trial Offer
145. Guarantee
146. Contests and Sweepstakes
147. Baking/Craft Ability
148. Lead Buying
149. Follow-Up
150. Tracking Plan
151. Marketing-on-Hold
152. Branded Entertainment
153. Product Placement
154. Radio Talk Show Guest
155. TV Talk Show Guest
156. Subliminal Marketing

COMPANY ATTRIBUTES

157. Proper View of Marketing
158. Brand Name Awareness
159. Positioning
160. Name
161. Memo
162. Theme Line
163. Writing Ability
164. Copywriting Ability
165. Headline Copy
166. Location

167. Hours of Operation
168. Days of Operation
169. Credit Cards Accepted
170. Financing Available
171. Credibility
172. Reputation
173. Efficiency
174. Quality
175. Service
176. Selection
177. Price
178. Opportunities to Upgrade
179. Referral Program
180. Spying
181. Testimonials
182. Extra Value
183. Adopt Noble Cause

COMPANY ATTITUDES

184. Easy To Do Business With
185. Honest Interest in People
186. Telephone Demeanor
187. Passion and Enthusiasm
188. Sensitivity
189. Patience

190. Flexibility
191. Generosity
192. Self Confidence
193. Neatness
194. Aggressiveness
195. Competitiveness
196. High Energy
197. Speed
198. Maintains Focus
199. Attention to Details
200. Takes Action

These 200 weapons should be considered for every guerrilla's arsenal. Once you've selected them, put them into a priority order, set a date for the launch of each weapon and appoint a person to mastermind your use of the weapons you've selected. Whatever you do, launch your guerrilla marketing attack LOGICALLY, only launching weapons when you can utilize them properly at a pace that is comfortable. KEEP TRACK because some things won't work, while others will. Unless you keep track, you won't know what is working and what is not. Guerrillas always know what is working and what is not. Some street team members will be valuable; others will waste your time, energy and money. Many concert attendees have learned that they can see shows for free by pre-

tending to be active street team members. You can eliminate this problem by requiring a digital photo of each poster before issuing tickets. By taking the time to carefully read progress reports and look at photos, the street team manager can fairly evaluate each member's performance and compensate them accordingly.

> *"Many street team members are going to miss the mark and, by casting a large net, one can balance out the 'failure factor' in the equation."*
>
> – Theresa Reed, Street Team Manager of High Sierra Music Festival and BEW Productions

GUERRILLA EXERCISE:

Review each weapon again and place it into one of four categories: using properly now, using but needs improvement, not using but should, not appropriate now. Your job is to work at your marketing plan to make the first category as lengthy as possible and to eliminate the second and third categories completely. Use different colored highlighters to assign each category a color.

Total the number of weapons in each category:

_____Weapons I use properly now

_____Weapons that need improvement

_____Weapons I don't use, but should

_____Weapons not appropriate right now

_____The total of all four categories

GUERRILLA ACTION STEPS:

A. List the weapons that need improvement

B. Make the improvement in your use of each of those weapons.

C. List the weapons you don't use, but should.

D. Launch each weapon you deem appropriate for your campaign at this time.

You need not utilize all 200 weapons, but you do need to improve the weapons requiring improvement, and you should be using all the weapons you believe can help increase your profits.

CHAPTER 4: Guerrilla Street Team Marketing Strategies

A Guerrilla Street Team Marketing strategy has only seven sentences. It is brief because it forces you to focus and because everyone in your organization can read and understand a simple strategy, putting everyone on the same wavelength. Some of the world's largest companies use seven-sentence strategies to guide their marketing efforts.

Let's say you manage a street team for a band that tours nationally. Let's say the name of your company is ProTeam Enterprises. And finally, let's say you have the mind of a guerrilla. Here's how a Guerrilla Street Team Marketing strategy would work for you:

1. The first sentence defines the purpose of your marketing.

"The purpose is to improve market visibility and recognition, to sell out all shows on summer tour and receive an average of five dollars in merchandise sales from each concert patron."

2. The second sentence defines how you'll achieve your purpose, concentrating on

your benefits and your competitive advantages.

"This will be accomplished by establishing a 'tour-friendly' route and schedule, providing an assortment of merchandise, and launching a well-planned Guerrilla Street Team Marketing attack by hiring an established Guerrilla Street Team Marketing firm. We will give away 20% of merchandise as promotional items in every major U.S. market."

3. The third sentence defines your target audience or audiences.

"Our target market is U.S. college students between the ages of 18 and 30; our secondary markets are college students in Japan and Denmark."

A demographic can be used to determine when and where advertising should be placed to achieve maximum results. Think about the following factors and try to relate them to your prospects:

Age, sex/gender, race/ethnicity, location of residence, socioeconomic status, religion, nationality, occupation, education, family size, marital status, ownership (home, car, motorcycle, pet, etc.), language, mobility, life cycles (fertility, mortality, migration).

Marketing researchers typically have two objectives: to determine what subgroups exist in the overall population and to create a picture of the characteristics of a typical member of each of these subgroups. Once these profiles are constructed, they can be used to develop a comprehensive Guerrilla Street Team Marketing strategy and plan.

4. The fourth sentence defines the marketing weapons you'll use.

"We will use a combination of direct mail and e-mail special offers, a website offering a free newsletter and contest, ads in newspapers, radio and television, and a Guerrilla Street Team Marketing attack that includes distributing 200 T-shirts and 5,000 CDs as promotional items."

5. The fifth sentence defines your niche in the market.

"We will position ourselves as the most exciting touring band in the country, offer benefits and free services to those on tour, sell a wide variety of merchandise, and build a strong relationship with our fan base by managing effective street teams."

6. The sixth sentence defines your identity.

"Our identity will be a blend of good music, stunning special effects, and close relationship with our fan base."

7. The seventh sentence defines your marketing budget as a percent of your projected gross sales.

"Ten percent of projected gross sales will be allocated to marketing."

This strategy should guide your efforts. Use it to measure ALL marketing materials you plan to use. Try to remain personally unattached to ideas, because if they do not fulfill your needs, you should forget them! You should review your strategy annually and make slight changes in it, especially in the fourth sentence. But the idea is to get it right the first time, then commit—making sure everyone on your team reads and understands this strategy.

- Postage machines may offer lower bulk rates and reduce labor costs by saving time
- Do your homework to find the lowest prices on shipping materials and promotional items by shopping around and negotiating
- When packaging a bulk mailing, form an assembly line to increase morale and productivity (have some drinks, turn up the music and rock out!)
- Recycle used mailing supplies (bubble wrap, boxes or anything reusable)

GUERRILLA EXERCISE:

Write a seven-sentence Guerrilla Street Team Marketing strategy for your project then apply it to your situation.

1. The purpose of my marketing is:

2. I will accomplish this purpose by:

3. My target audience is:

4. Marketing weapons I plan to employ are:

5. My niche in the marketplace is:

6. My business identity is:

7. I plan to devote ____ percent of gross sales to Guerrilla Street Team Marketing.

GUERRILLA ACTION STEPS:

A. Show your completed strategy to people in your organization who are involved with marketing.

B. Show your completed strategy to each of your band mates or associates, even if they are not involved with your marketing.

C. Give your plan life by doing exactly what you say you will and measuring all your marketing materials, current and future, against the strategy. If they do not follow the strategy, change or discard them.

CHAPTER 5: Guerrilla Street Team Marketing Personality Traits

From ancient Greek philosophers to modern musical icons, all successful people share certain personality traits. There are now many books and programs that pave the road to personal and financial success by explaining that if you mirror certain fundamental personality traits that successful people share, you too will be successful.

Here are eight personality traits that good street team managers possess:

1. **PATIENCE:** This trait is the most important by far.

2. **IMAGINATION:** This doesn't necessarily refer to headlines, graphics, jingles or being clever. If you're going to send a newsletter, recognize that everyone sends newsletters. Why should anyone read yours? Make it special and imaginative. Put coupons in it. Give people an incentive to read it from beginning to end.

3. **SENSITIVITY:** People who run first-rate marketing shows are sensitive to their market, their prospects, the economy, the community and the competition.

4. **EGO STRENGTH:** The first people who will tire of your marketing program will be your co-workers, followed closely by the band and their families and friends. They will counsel you to change because they are bored. Remember that your prospects are not bored and have barely heard of you. Your supporters will not be bored and will forever read your marketing materials because they still support you.

5. **AGGRESSIVENESS:** You need to be aggressive in your spending and thinking. When you hear that a competing band, event, product or venue has a mailing list of 4,000, you want 40,000!

6. **CONSTANT LEARNING:** Continuing your education will ensure that you are achieving your potential with the most innovative and modern resources.

7. **GENEROSITY:** Guerrillas view marketing as an opportunity to help their prospects and customers succeed at their goals, whatever they may be. They are generous with their time, their information and think of things they can give away to help those people.

8. **TAKE ACTION**: Many industry professionals read books, listen to tapes, take courses and attend seminars and panel discussions. But most of them

keep this information to themselves. Guerrillas learn in the very same ways, but take action based upon what they have learned. They know that action is the real power behind Guerrilla Marketing. It all comes down to knowing how to hustle!

Those are the eight traits that great marketing directors seem to have in common. Now, let's examine the traits of an effective street team member.

Here are some actual e-mail responses to a street team invitation. This is the first e-mail from a street team member who proved to be most reliable (pay close attention to grammar and slang):

> *Hey, what's up? Saw your post on the net today, figured I'd shoot you an e-mail. I do all the Philly shows. I can provide references if necessary, they'll tell you what's up. So basically, for everyone's benefit get me involved.*
>
> *John Doe*
>
> *531 Any St*
>
> *Philadelphia, PA 19128*
>
> ###.###.####

John's writing style is personal and relaxed. He is confident and concise. Experienced street team members will usually provide their contact information in their initial e-mail.

Here's another promising initial e-mail response from a quality prospect:

I am a Music Management Student in Hartford and am very interested in helping promote the show here tomorrow night. I am planning on attending and would be happy to help put up some flyers and spread the word. If there is still time for me to collect and put up posters please let me know!

Jane Doe

Hartford, CT

P.S. I am also a current intern at a local music venue and would be able to help spread word in the NYC area as well. I look forward to hearing from you! Thank you – Jane

Here is a simply written response from another reliable street team member:

Hi! Holli here... Happy Friday to ya!

I just wanted to check in about being part of your street team, if there is anything I can do, or should do. Just let me know! Hope all is well!

Talk with you soon.

Much love,

Holli Doe:)

Many street team members use lots of slang and symbols and will talk to you like a friend, so don't think that professional writing skills or smiley faces completely determine street team members' effectiveness. You'll find that poor grammar, lack of contact information and being generally clueless is indicative of slackness.

Here are some responses from average, underachieving street team members:

- *I plan on attending alot of those show and alot of the festis. I would also like to say that im very interested in the lineup of this years festis, and would love to volunteer at your fine festival. Do i need to talk with anyone in order for me to do that? I looking forward to receiving a return response. THANK YOU*
- *I'm not sure when you are coming to my town, I haven't checked my email lately. Anytime you guys want my help and I am in the vicinity I will gladly put the word out. -Janet Doe, Nashville TN*

- *Yo yo! Sign me up for the street team. Im always up for spreading the word. Would love to hear some tunes from the band if you have something to send as well. peaz!*
- *Sure, I'll help promote y'all... When will you be in the area and where are you playing? I am co-producing a massive fund raising event on June 11. I will be doing lots of promoting this month anyway . One Love Janice Doe*

> *There are so many people who sign up for the team and I never hear from them. I know they still read our e-mails because they will reply to an e-mail and ask something totally random or ask to be "guest listed" for a show. It's difficult to tell if street teamers are actually going out and promoting! Dealing with all the bullshit is part of the job.*
>
> – Stephanie Shoulders, Street Team/E-Team Marketing Coordinator of Century Media Records

As you can see, knowing the difference between a quality prospect and an average under-achiever can mean the difference between failure and success for your project. Although writing styles are not completely definitive, they do provide a certain amount of insight into each street team member's skill set and personality.

GUERRILLA EXERCISE:

Compare the eight guerrilla personality traits with your own, and then be honest in knowing which ones you must develop even more.

Put a checkmark next to each of the Guerrilla Marketing personality characteristics that you possess.

- Patience
- Imagination
- Sensitivity
- Ego Strength
- Aggressiveness
- Constant learning
- Generosity
- Take action

GUERRILLA ACTION STEPS:

A. Circle each personality trait that does not have a checkmark.

B. Begin developing those traits in yourself.

C. Put a checkmark next to each trait that you are able to develop.

CHAPTER 6: Guerrilla Street Team Marketing Attack

Succeeding in the music industry with a Guerilla Street Team Marketing attack is a 10-step process. Take all 10 steps and watch your fan base grow! Your ticket, album and merchandise sales are GUARANTEED to increase exponentially if you follow every guideline in this book!

1. The first step is to **research** everything you can. That means carefully investigating your market, your product or service, your competition, your industry and your options in media. It means looking into your amazement factor, into the latest technology and market trends, and into the makeup of your existing fans.

What media reaches your target audience? What media makes them respond and buy? Should you focus on advertising, direct marketing or a combination? Do you need a database, and if so, why? There are answers to these questions and guerrillas will find them. Your time in research will pay off.

2. The second step is to **write a benefits list**. Have a meeting. Invite your key personnel and at least one patron—because patrons have seen your show, bought the T-shirt and will be back next year. They

are tuned in to aspects that you may not even consider to be benefits. For example, a festival patron may refuse to return to an event if they have recurring negative portable toilet experiences.

Meeting Tips:

- Have your support staff meeting in a neutral space because it will encourage creativity and boost morale
- Never reject an idea until the next meeting; think about it and write down your reactions and suggestions
- Only positive minds can recharge each other. Avoid thinking and saying anything negative. Get away from negative people or remove them from your group.

3. Step number three is to **select the weapons you'll use.** In Chapter Three, I listed 200 weapons from which you may make your selection. Use as

many weapons as you can. More than 50 of the 200 are free. After you've selected the weaponry, put the weapons into priority order. Next to each weapon, write the name of the person who is in charge of masterminding the use of the weapon plus the date it will be launched. Consider each date to be a promise to yourself; guerrillas do not lie to themselves, so be realistic.

4. The fourth step is to **create a Guerrilla Street Team Marketing strategy**.

5. Step five is to **make a Guerrilla Street Team Marketing calendar**. Keep detailed records of things you plan to do and have done. Then, base your plans on what you know about the past and expect to see in the future.

6. Step six is to **locate fusion marketing partners** like record labels and bands with the same fans and the same standards as you have. Offer to go in on co-marketing ventures with them. Trade newsletter lists and links online.

7. Step seven is to **launch your attack at a comfortable pace.** You need to very honest with yourself on this one. Be realistic about finances, work and family needs, and your place in the market.

8. The eighth step, and this is a tough one, is to **maintain the attack**. The first seven steps are extremely simple compared to this step. Maintaining the attack means sticking with your plan. Everyone wants success to come instantly, but it doesn't happen that way.

Tenacity vs. Stupidity: Know the Difference

Be realistic; know when to change your plans.

9. Step nine is to **keep track**. Some of your weapons will hit the mark. Other will miss completely. How will you know which is which? By asking customers where they heard of you. By finding out what made them contact you. Keeping track is difficult, but necessary. If you aren't ready to keep track, you aren't ready to launch your attack.

Tips for Quantifying Your Results:

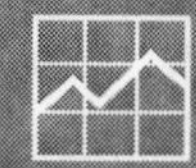

- Organize your e-mail by using folders and mailing lists
- Customize street team invitations' subject lines to quantify responses from different markets
- Create different e-mail addresses for different offers, giveaways and special promotions
- Use the latest technology and specialty products/services like iPods, MySpace, Fancorps and Dropcards

10. The 10 and final step is to **improve** in all areas: your message, the marketing weapons you're using and your results. A Guerrilla Street Team Marketing attack is a never-ending process.

That's it! Ten steps to succeeding with a Guerrilla Street Team Marketing attack. If it sounds easy, reread this lesson. It works, but it's not easy.

The real secret to succeeding in the music industry is never giving up!

GUERRILLA EXERCISE:

Take the first five steps right now. Begin to take the sixth. Then, you'll be positioned for success from the start. Putting your attack into writing with this exercise will give wings to your dreams.

Check each step of the Guerrilla Street Team Marketing attack that you have taken or will take:

- I have done the proper research.
- I have written a benefits list.
- I have selected the weapons I will employ.
- I have written my strategy.
- I have prepared my calendar.
- I have located marketing partners.
- I have launched my attack at a comfortable pace.
- I am able to maintain my attack.
- I am able to keep track of each weapon's effectiveness.
- I have improved each facet of my attack.

GUERRILLA ACTION STEPS:

A. Review where you put checkmarks on the checklist above and circle the statements at which no checkmark appears. These are the areas that you must focus upon to succeed with your attack. Watch out for them!

B. Decide on the specific actions you will take for each statement so as to mount an effective Guerrilla Street Team Marketing attack. List these in the space provided beneath each statement for which you have circled the number.

C. Take the actions you have listed, one by one, until each of the statements merit a checkmark. An incomplete attack is a recipe for failure.

BONUS MATERIAL

WHAT DO OTHER STREET TEAM MARKETING PROFESSIONALS THINK IS THE MOST IMPORTANT THING ABOUT MANAGING A STREET TEAM?

Tom Russell, National Promotions Director for Superfly Productions, believes, "Communication. In order to manage a successful street team program, it is essential that the street team coordinator be in constant communication with his/her team. This communication is key, as it helps one:

- Check on the progress of the street team member's work
- Get Feedback from them on how their work was received by general public
- Develop a more personal working relationship with the street team member
- Guide and control how the street team member uses his/her time and labor

Many street team captains/coordinators never meet street team members face to face, so constant communication via phone or e-mail is the only way to really manage a street team effectively."

Superfly Productions' events include: Bonnaroo and many more. To learn more about Superfly Productions visit them on the web at:

www.superflypresents.com

Lisa Cyr, Street Team Coordinator for AC Entertainment says, "In my experience, the most important thing about managing a street team is building solid relationships not only with the street team members, but also between them. I believe that the love of music initially inspires people to join a street team, but what keeps certain people motivated is more than just free tickets and swag. Knowing that they [street team members] will be working with people they have bonded with is definitely a motivating factor in the amount they choose to participate. As a result, I think it's important to schedule times for everyone to get together when we are not working. This lets people get to know each other and makes it more fun to work with them at upcoming shows. Putting things on a more personal level inspires people to help more. Everyone is more willing to help when it's a friend."

AC Entertainment produces several concerts and events, including Bonnaroo. To learn more about AC Entertainment, visit them on the web at:

www.acentertainment.com

Theresa Reed, Street Team Manager for The High Sierra Music Festival and BEW Productions, states that, "It is a tie between acknowledging your street team members' hard work and aiming high. Many street team members are going to miss the mark and, by casting a large net, one can balance out the "failure factor" in the equation. There are so many ways to thank street teamers, two minutes of your time can create a memory that will last a lifetime for them!"

To learn more about the High Sierra Music Festival and BEW Productions, visit them on the web at:

www.highsierramusic.com

and **www.garajmahal.com**

James M. Aquafredda, National Managing Director of Street Team Promotion, observes, "Leadership is #1. Getting the best from people who may have never seen their own "best" before. Leadership is also the key component in managing a street team effectively because the nature of street team promotion in many cases requires a leader to make key decisions regarding field staff that can dramatically alter performance and the success of a campaign, or lack thereof. Good leaders execute great campaigns. Poor leadership trickles down to the staff one way or another and can directly impact campaigns results."

Street Team Promotion's clients include: Warner Brothers Pictures, Verizon, WWF, *The Washington Post*, NBC Universal, ABC, Stonyfield Farm, Walt Disney, Major League Soccer, Kraft, Post, H&R Block and Univision. To learn more about Street Team Promotion, visit them on the web at:

www.streetteampromotion.com

Stephanie Shoulders, Street Team/E-Team Marketing Coordinator for Century Media Records, says, "It's hard to find dedicated people that really want to help out for the bands' sake. There are so many people who sign up for the team and I never hear from them. What's the point of that? The funny thing is that I know they still read our e-mails, because every once in awhile they will reply to an e-mail and ask about something totally random or ask to be "guest listed" for a show. It's difficult to tell sometimes if street teamers are actually going out and promoting!

More and more we require photos of people holding up the swag outside of a show or of the teamer passing out the swag. This way we know that the packages we send aren't just sitting under someone's bed or popping up on eBay! There are some really great people we get to work with which really keeps you motivated!

Dealing with all the bullshit is part of the job. I think it's tough to stay positive when you're consistently asking people to spend their own time promoting something for free. We have prizes of course, but that's for people who are really showing us they are out their busting their asses for the bands. It's also really annoying to deal with people who just want tons of free stuff. It's not fair to the rest of the people who are working hard and it just seems ungrateful. Another thing we struggle with is getting enough materials to promote or giveaway for prizes. I always try and find anything extra we can get that's special for the team, or I spend my own time driving out to a video shoot or something to get posters or CDs for the team signed. But, most importantly, we want the teamers to know they we really appreciate what they are doing for the bands, and that the bands really appreciate them as well."

To learn more about Century Media Records, visit them on the web at:

www.centurymedia.com

Matt Hogan, Marketing Director of SCI Fidelity Records/Madison House Presents, writes, "In my experience, the most important part of running an effective street team is building relationships. The people who volunteer to help support their favorite band are doing it for the love of the music, and since there is none of the accountability normally associated with a paid position, it's critical that you build solid relationships with your best street teamers, and truly make them feel as though they are a valued part of the team (which they most certainly are).

Finding good, reliable street teamers can be challenging, and retaining them for any significant period of time is even more difficult. They are generally in cities and towns hundreds or thousands of miles away, so there's usually no way to physically check up on their efforts. You have to trust that they're really doing the work they say they're doing, and that the promo materials you send aren't going to waste. So, it's key that you maintain regular communication with your team and respond to their e-mails as often as possible, and as personally as you can, to try and get a sense of what they're about and what their level of commitment/responsibility is. Also, whenever possible, I try to arrange face-to-face meetings with our street teamers at shows and festivals, so I can look them in the eye, give them a hug and thank them in person. Not only does this allow you to get a better sense of who you're dealing with, but it puts a face to the anonymous e-mails that we normally use to communicate with our street team. People are much more likely to follow through on promo for someone they've met personally (and might even consider to be a friend), versus a nameless/faceless entity.

And in terms of rewards for the street team, getting a spot on the guest list only goes so far, especially when you're talking about young bands that only charge $10 at the door. So, you need to let these people feel as though they are a part of something larger, and that they are getting something valuable in return for their time and effort. Sometimes this can be their first experience in the music business. Often, you can illustrate to them how they are contributing to the overall community in a positive way, and helping the scene to grow. But any time you can go above and beyond and give them something you can't put a price tag on—a signed CD or poster, a VIP or after-show pass, a chance to meet their favorite musician face-to-face—you're going to get a much better response, and you'll have far greater follow-through and loyalty from your street team.

The passion of your fan base can be the most effective and inexpensive means of promoting your band. Don't take this for granted, and do everything you can to capitalize on (and maximize) the grassroots buzz that is already out there happening. Peer-to-peer communication is far more powerful than standard print/internet advertising, and should be utilized as such."

Artists include: The String Cheese Incident, Keller Williams, Umphrey's McGee, the Disco Biscuits, Railroad Earth, Tea Leaf Green, The Greyboy Allstars, Steve Kimock Band, Brothers Past. To learn more about Madison House Presents, visit them on the web at:

www.madisonhouseinc.com

G.I. Sanders, Marketing Coordinator of Fancorps, claims, "By far the most important part of managing a street team is communication—not only from the team leader to the members but between the members themselves. It's no different than a football "team"; there must be open lines of communication on several levels for any kind of "team" to function and be successful. We provide many ways for the team to keep informed like messaging, forums, chat rooms, orders, news, etc. To learn more about Fancorps, visit them on the web at:

www.fancorps.com

Danny Ornelas, National Director of Marketing of MySpace Records, thinks, "The most important thing about managing a street team is getting as many eyeballs as possible—this can be done in a million different ways. First, determine your target audience (very important!). Second, research what sites they frequent, what bands they like and hit them up at these shows, where they shop, where they eat, where they go to school, etc. Find out everything about your target audience, and then get your information into their hands."

Artists include: Mickey Avalon, Hollywood Undead, Kate Voegele and Sherwood. To learn more about MySpace Records, visit them on the web at:

www.myspace.com/myspacerecords.com

J. Nadolny, Systems Account Coordinator of GMR Marketing, writes, "I would say have patience and to not take things personally. There are a lot of people who sign up to be involved you never hear from again; you have to let it roll off your back. Lead by example ... I know of some street team leaders who never even go out and hang a poster themselves, I think it is great to go out with the teams if possible and show that you are not afraid to sweat and be a part of the team. It's not just sitting at a desk and sending out packages!"

Clients include: Visa, Alltel, American Eagle Outfitters, Axe, Best Buy, Amgen, Microsoft, Miller, Mercedes-Benz, Mercury, Major League Baseball, New Balance, Wrigley, Motorola, Power Bar, Daimler Chrysler, Lowe's, Pepsi, Intel, McDonald's, ESPN, HD DVD. To learn more about GMR Marketing, visit them on the web at:

www.gmrmarketing.com

Brian Asplin, Founder of Harmonized Records/Macro-Management and Publicity, responds, "The most important thing about managing a street team is to know your strengths in each market, to be aware of your leaders and who to call on when you need serious work on a show. Identifying these folks and empowering them is one of the best things you can do for your team."

Artists include: Lotus, EOTO, Hot Buttered Rum, STRUT, Barefoot Manner, The Afromotive, The Barrel House Mamas, Telepath, Pnuma Trio, The Mayhem String Band, RAQ, The Carolina Chocolate Drops, DJ Williams, Infradig, Mecca Bodega, The Motet, Cadillac Jones, The Recipe and ulu. To learn more about Harmonized Records and Macro-Management and Publicity, visit them on the web at:

www.harmonizedrecords.com

and **www.macro-management.com**

Seth Weiner, Founder of Shimon Presents Inc., writes, "One of the most important things about managing a street team is to personally know who is on your team. Building a good relationship with strong communication is key. We do our best to have a street team leader in each market that can oversee the team members as well as having an employee manage each street team from our office. It is hard to really tell if a team member is doing their work, but when you add in a personal touch, where our team manager gets on the phone with the team leaders in addition to meeting them in person when possible, the team is more likely to get the job done.

Artists include: Perpetual Groove, The Toasters, New Monsoon, New Rider's of the Purple Sage, Moonshine Still, The Jason "Lefty" Williams Band, Blue Turtle Seduction, The Bridge, Yo Mama's Big Fat Booty Band. Events: All Good Music Festival, Jam in the Dam, Langerado, Camp Bisco, and Jam Cruise. To learn more about Shimon Presents, visit them on the web at:

www.shimonpresents.com

About the Authors

ABOUT THE AUTHORS

Brad Lovejoy grew up in a peaceful and beautiful setting—rural West Virginia—and attended his first three years of college at WVU. He played in rock, jam and bluegrass bands throughout his early twenties and worked several (fun, but low-paying) jobs such as whitewater river guide, horseback trail guide, carpenter's assistant, restaurant server and cook—anything that would allow him to stay out late and gig on the weekends. Particularly found of outdoor music festivals, he has spent every summer since 1998 working in different areas of festival production and marketing. Lovejoy took on music industry roles such as college radio host, street team manager, stage manager, assistant production manager, music conference panelist and author. He and his wife, Michelle, moved to Asheville, NC in 2006. Lovejoy is currently working at The Mountain Xpress, an alternative newsweekly, as Assistant Distribution Manager.

Lovejoy decided to write The Guerrilla Street Team Marketing Guide when he researched street team marketing and found very little about the subject. Live marketing and peer-to-peer marketing are dominating the alternative lifestyle markets and he wanted to illuminate this vague subject. The music industry is becoming more accessable by the minute and grassroots marketing is one of the only ways beginning artists can gain a presence in the marketplace. In addition to the music industry, the same tactics that work for bands will work for any business. Lovejoy knows that there is enough business for everyone and wants to help those who are trying to help themselves.

Jay Conrad Levinson is the author of the best-selling marketing series in history, "Guerrilla Marketing," plus 39 other business books. His books have sold 14 million copies worldwide. And his guerrilla concepts have influenced marketing so much that his books appear in 41 languages and are required reading in MBA programs worldwide.

Jay taught Guerrilla Marketing for ten years at the extension division of the University of California in Berkeley. He was a practitioner of it in the Un ited States -- as Senior VP at J. Walter Thompson, and in Europe, as Creative Director of Leo Burnett Advertising.

A winner of first prizes in all the media, he has been part of the creative teams that made household names of The Marlboro Man, The Pillsbury Doughboy, Allstate's good hands, United's friendly skies, and the Sears Diehard battery.

Jay has written for *Entrepreneur Magazine, Inc. Magazine*, and the Microsoft Website, as well as numerous other publications. He is the Chairman of Guerrilla Marketing International. His Guerrilla Marketing is series of books, workshops, CDs, DVD's, an Internet website, and The Guerrilla Marketing Association -- a marketing support system for small business.

FREE BONUS!

FREE BONUS!

The Winner of the Street Team Makeover Contest Will Receive $4,000 Worth of Marketing Tools!

Act Now! Enter the "Win a Street Team Makeover Contest" by visiting:

www.guerrillastreetteam.com

Here's what you'll get:

- 1 year of videoconference consulting from author Brad Lovejoy: A $2500 value!

  We will assess the current situation and make a 1-year Guerrilla Street Team Marketing Strategy. From there, we'll brainstorm and create a detailed Guerrilla Street Team Marketing Calendar. Encouraging creativity, setting realistic goals and measuring performance against expectations will ensure a successful campaign for any band at any level.

- A One Year "Premium" subscription to Fancorps - meaning we'll give away the Brigade account for one year: A $1250 value!

Fancorps: Utilizing the best in Web 2.0 features, Fancorps provides countless communication tools for an artist, label, manager, or company to organize and manage a street team. Fancorps gives you numerous ways to communicate with your team. Private Messaging, Forums, Comments, News and Events are just a few of the ways you can use Fancorps to keep your members informed and up to date with the latest information.

Fancorps encourages the team to communicate with each other as well, and the more the better as everything done within the site is tracked and team members are rewarded with points for all participation.

It's simple, you may have thousands of friends on Myspace, but how many of them are actually working for you? Can you easily track what they do? Can you contact them in groups based on their participation level or location? Didn't think so. Fancorps is designed for your hardcore fan base, the fans who truly want to help you out, NOT the casual fan who might add any number of bands on Myspace to their friend's list. If a team member isn't working for you on a daily/weekly basis they will automatically be deleted from your team. This streamlines your team for you, keeping around only those who are actually helping out.

- 500 custom-printed Dropcards: A $250 value!

Dropcards: Upload your card artwork and we'll print and ship you high quality plastic download cards with a unique Access Code on the back along with the URL where the cardholder can redeem the card. Sell or distribute your cards! The cardholder will log on to your website and enter their card's Access Code to download your media successfully bridging the gap between the physical and digital world.

To ensure that you get the most out of your brand, Dropcards offers a broad suite of digital resources to help strengthen your niche in the consumer marketplace.

With millions of songs, ringtones, movies, magazines and gifts to choose from, Dropcards blends the best parts of traditional marketing with the power and flexibility of online promotions.

Music Download Cards . Ringtone Cards . Custom Content Promotions . Sweepstakes. Mobile/SMS promotions . Content Acquisition . Web Development.

To learn more about the many ways Dropcards can increase your brand awareness and strengthen consumer relationships, please visit www.dropcards.com.

W9-BRA-013

Henry and the Clubhouse

by Beverly Cleary

illustrated by Louis Darling

A YEARLING BOOK

A YEARLING BOOK
Published by
Dell Publishing Co., Inc.
1 Dag Hammarskjold Plaza
New York, New York 10017

Copyright © 1962 by Beverly Cleary

All rights reserved. For information address William Morrow & Company, Inc., New York, New York 10016.

Yearling ® TM 913705, Dell Publishing Co., Inc.

ISBN: 0-440-43305-3

Printed in the United States of America

Reprinted by arrangement with William Morrow & Company, New York

Fourteenth Dell printing—January 1985

CW

HENRY AND THE CLUBHOUSE

OTHER YEARLING BOOKS YOU WILL ENJOY:

HENRY HUGGINS, *Beverly Cleary*
HENRY AND BEEZUS, *Beverly Cleary*
HENRY AND THE PAPER ROUTE, *Beverly Cleary*
HENRY AND RIBSY, *Beverly Cleary*
RIBSY, *Beverly Cleary*
THE MOUSE AND THE MOTORCYCLE, *Beverly Cleary*
RALPH S. MOUSE, *Beverly Cleary*
RUNAWAY RALPH, *Beverly Cleary*
OTIS SPOFFORD, *Beverly Cleary*
BEEZUS AND RAMONA, *Beverly Cleary*

YEARLING BOOKS are designed especially to entertain and enlighten young people. Charles F. Reasoner, Professor Emeritus of Children's Literature and Reading, New York University, is consultant to this series.

For a complete listing of all Yearling titles, write to Dell Publishing Co., Inc., Promotion Department, P.O. Box 3000, Pine Brook, N.J. 07058.

Table of Contents

HENRY AND THE CLUBHOUSE

CHAPTER ONE

Henry Goes for a Ride

HENRY HUGGINS had a lot of good ideas that fall when he first had his paper route, but somehow his ideas had a way of not turning out as he had planned. Something always went wrong.

There was, for example, that Saturday afternoon in October, when Henry found himself with nothing to do until it was time to start delivering *Journals*. Naturally he wandered into the kitchen and opened the refrigerator to see what he could find. At the sound of the door opening, his dog Ribsy and his cat Nosy came running in case he should be planning to feed them.

"Henry, you just ate lunch," said Mrs. Huggins, who had washed her son's slacks and was now struggling to shove metal stretchers into the legs. "Can't you find something to do instead of opening the refrigerator every five minutes?"

"I'm thinking, Mom," answered Henry. He was thinking that he would like to build something, some kind of a house. A doghouse, a tree house or a clubhouse. A tree house would be pretty hard, but he was sure he could build a doghouse or a clubhouse. All he needed was lumber and nails.

"Well, think with the refrigerator door shut," suggested Mrs. Huggins with a smile. She had succeeded in stretching Henry's slacks and now she leaned them, tight on their frames, against the sink. "And *please* find something to do."

"O.K., Mom," said Henry, and walked out the back door in search of something to keep him busy. He considered. He could go over to the Quimbys' house and play checkers with Beezus, a girl whose real name was Beatrice, but her pesty little sister Ramona would probably spoil the game. He could go see if his friend Murph, who was the smartest boy in the whole school, was building anything interesting in his garage. Or he could try to sell subscriptions to the *Journal*. That was what he should do, but somehow Henry was not anxious to start ringing strange doorbells. No, what he really wanted to do was build something. He decided to scout around Klickitat Street and see if he could find enough boards for a doghouse. That would be the easiest to build and would not take much lumber.

As Henry walked around the side of his house, he noticed his next-door neighbor's car parked on the driveway with a U-Haul-It trailer attached.

Now that was interesting, thought Henry. What was Hector Grumbie going to haul?

The front door of the Grumbies' house opened, and Mr. Grumbie appeared to be coming out backwards. This was even more interesting. Why didn't Mr. Grumbie walk out frontwards? Bit by bit more of his neighbor appeared, and Henry saw that he was tugging at something.

Henry decided he had better investigate. From the Grumbies' front walk he discovered that Mr. Grumbie was pulling and Mrs. Grumbie was pushing a bathtub out of the house. They were sliding it across the floor on an old blanket.

Mr. Grumbie paused to wipe his forehead. "Whew!" he exclaimed. "These old bathtubs were built like battleships."

"May I help?" Henry asked eagerly. After all, his mother wanted him to find something to do.

"Sure," said Mr. Grumbie. "You can get on the other end and help push."

Henry ran up the steps, and because the bathtub was blocking the door, he climbed into it, out the other side, and joined Mrs. Grumbie in pushing.

Henry was secretly wondering, but was too polite to ask, if the Grumbies were planning to give up bathing. Instead he inquired, "What are you going to do with it?"

"Take it to the dump," answered Mr. Grumbie, "unless you would like to have it. We are remodeling the bathroom and have to get rid of it to make room for the new tub, which will be delivered Monday."

Henry thought it over. There were all sorts of interesting things he could do with a bathtub in his back yard. Wash his dog Ribsy in it, cool off in it himself on a hot day, bob for apples at Halloween. Build a clubhouse around it if he had that much lumber. All sorts of things. A bathtub in the yard would be much more fun than a tub in the bathroom, but Henry was sure his mother would not feel the same way about it.

"No, thank you, Mr. Grumbie," Henry said with regret and then he had a better idea. The new bathtub would come in a crate and perhaps Mr. Grumbie would let him have the boards to build a doghouse.

By that time several neighbors had come over to the Grumbies' to watch. Even Ribsy had taken an interest and had come down from the Huggins' doormat where he had been napping. Mr. Grumbie tied a rope around the tub and with the help of Henry and the bystanders who hung onto the rope, eased the tub, bump-bump-bump, down the front steps, slid it across the lawn, and then boosted it onto the trailer, where Mr. Grumbie tied it securely.

"Want to go for a ride to the dump?" Mr. Grumbie asked Henry.

The dump! Immediately Henry pictured a fascinating jumble of old bathtubs, washing machines, tires, and baby buggies. There was no telling what he might find at the dump. There might even be some old boards he could bring home.

"Can I ride in the bathtub?" he asked eagerly.

"Sure." Mr. Grumbie was agreeable. "Go ask your mother."

Henry ran to the open kitchen window. "Hey, Mom! Mr. Grumbie wants me to ride to the dump with him. Can I go?"

"All right, Henry." Mrs. Huggins' voice came through the window.

"Come on, Ribsy!" Henry bounded across the lawn and climbed into the bathtub. Ribsy scrambled in behind him.

"All set?" asked Mr. Grumbie, opening the door of his car.

"All set," answered Henry, and Mr. Grumbie maneuvered the car and trailer down the driveway and into the street.

Riding in a bathtub, which of course had no springs or upholstery, was bumpy, but Henry did not care. No one else in the neighborhood had ever gone for a ride in a bathtub. He shouted and waved to his friends Scooter and Robert, who were playing catch on the sidewalk. They stared after him in surprise. Ribsy put his paws on the edge of the tub and barked.

When Mr. Grumbie stopped at the first stop sign, Henry saw his friend Beezus and her little sister Ramona, who had a lot of string stuck to her chin with Scotch tape. Henry guessed she was trying to copy one of the many disguises of Sheriff Bud on television. Ramona never missed the Sheriff Bud program.

"Hi!" called Henry.

"Hello, Henry." Beezus looked with admiration

at Henry in the bathtub. He could tell she wished she could go for a ride in a bathtub too.

Ramona scowled ferociously and pointed straight at Henry. "Remember—only *you* can prevent forest fires."

Henry ignored Ramona. He knew she was only repeating what she had heard Smokey Bear say on television all summer. "So long!" he called to Beezus as Mr. Grumbie drove on.

Ribsy, tired of barking over the edge of the tub, curled up and tried to go to sleep, but whenever the trailer went over a bump, he lifted his head and looked annoyed. In the bathtub little bumps felt like big bumps. They rumbled and bumped down Klickitat Street to a main thoroughfare, and then Henry had an idea. He was the president of the United States riding in a parade! He sat up straight in the bathtub, nodding and waving and doffing an imaginary hat. Mr. Grumbie's car became a column of tanks preceding him down the

avenue, and one airplane in the sky became a formation of fighter planes overhead. Henry could practically hear the cheers of the throngs crowded along the curbs to watch his journey to the White House.

Henry did in fact hear a few real cheers, or perhaps jeers was a better word, mostly from boys along the way.

"Hey! Don't forget to wash your back!"

"Be careful! Don't step on the soap!"

With great dignity Henry nodded and waved. A great man on his way to the White House could afford to ignore such people, especially when he was surrounded by Secret Service men.

Henry was having too much fun to act dignified very long. He saw several boys standing in front of a bicycle shop and could not resist waving and shouting, "Hats off! The flag is passing by!"

"Boo!" yelled the boys. "Boo! Boo!" They held their noses and waved Henry on down the street.

Ribsy scrambled to his feet and barked over the edge of the tub. Henry, who was the kind of man who *would* take his dog to the White House, folded his arms and grinned in a superior manner, because he was riding in the bathtub and the boys were standing on the sidewalk. The afternoon had turned out better than he had expected, and he still had the dump to look forward to.

And then Henry passed a *Journal* truck heading in the opposite direction. Suddenly he was no longer president of the United States. He was no longer interested in lumber for a doghouse. He was plain Henry Huggins, a boy who had completely forgotten that he had forty-three papers to deliver this afternoon. This was terrible! If he did not get those papers delivered, his route might be taken away from him before he had had it a month. Then, because he was the youngest *Journal* carrier in the neighborhood, Mr. Capper, who was the district manager, and everyone else, would say he was not old enough to handle a route. And that would be about the worst thing that could possibly happen. He would never live it down.

"Mr. Grumbie! Mr. Grumbie!" yelled Henry, but Mr. Grumbie drove on down the street unaware that he was carrying his passenger farther and farther from his paper route.

"Mr. Grumbie! Mr. Grumbie!" There was no response but the bump and rattle of the trailer. Henry was trapped in a bathtub in the middle of Lombard Street. "Mr. Grumbie! Mr. Grumbie!"

At the next stop sign Henry stood up in the bathtub and frantically waved both hands, hoping to attract Mr. Grumbie's attention in the rear view mirror.

It worked, because Mr. Grumbie stuck his head out the window and called, "Something wrong back there?"

"My route!" yelled Henry. "I forgot my paper route!"

The signal changed and cars and trucks began to honk. Mr. Grumbie, in the center lane of traffic, had to drive on.

Henry sat down with a bump. The Saturday afternoon traffic was heavy and it would be difficult for Mr. Grumbie to change lanes while pulling a trailer. They were still in the center lane when they came to the next stop sign.

"I'll pull over as soon as I can," Mr. Grumbie called back to Henry.

Henry now felt ridiculous sitting in the bathtub in the middle of a heavily traveled street. He wondered why he had thought riding in a tub would be fun in the first place. A boy who was old enough to have a paper route was too old to do such a silly thing. Cross street after cross street went by and Henry was carried farther and farther from his route. By this time the other boys were counting and folding their papers and Mr. Capper was probably wondering what had happened to Henry, the youngest carrier. Maybe Mr. Capper was already wondering what boy could take over Henry's route. Maybe he was saying to Scooter and the other boys, "I'm afraid Henry isn't old enough to handle a route. Do you know any older boy who could take his place?" It was not a happy prospect.

A gap appeared in the right-hand lane of traffic and Mr. Grumbie eased his car and the trailer into it. There was a solid line of cars parked along the curb, and no place to stop. Another block went by. Still there was no place where Mr. Grumbie could stop. Henry caught a glimpse of a clock inside a dry-cleaning shop. Four thirty-five. He would never get to the district manager's garage and get his papers folded and delivered by six o'clock.

Mr. Grumbie signaled and made a right turn into a service station. Henry, followed by Ribsy, scrambled out of the bathtub as Mr. Grumbie got out of his car.

"I'm sure sorry I forgot about my route," Henry apologized.

"What are we going to do about it?" asked Mr. Grumbie. "I can't turn around and take you home now, because the dump closes at five and I've got to get rid of this tub this week end. Besides, I am renting the trailer by the hour and I want to get it back as soon as I can."

"That's all right," said Henry. "I have enough money for bus fare."

"Do you know the way home?" asked Mr. Grumbie.

"Sure. I can catch the bus across the street and I know where to transfer to the other bus." Henry was eager to be on his way.

"O.K.," agreed Mr. Grumbie, and climbed back into his car.

"Wait!" yelled Henry as Mr. Grumbie started to drive off. "Ribsy! Can you take Ribsy with you? I can't take him on the bus."

Across the street a bus pulled up to the stop,

discharged a passenger and departed with a puff of exhaust.

"I guess so. Come on, pooch." Mr. Grumbie opened the rear door of his car and Henry shoved Ribsy inside and slammed the door. He knew from past experience that a dog was not allowed on a bus unless it was in a box tied shut. Henry had enough problems without searching for a box.

When Mr. Grumbie drove off, Henry waited for the traffic light to change from red to green before he crossed the street to the bus stop. He had just missed a bus, he knew, and as he wondered how long he would have to wait for the next bus, he fingered the change in the pocket of his jeans. Bus fare and a dime left over. Enough for one telephone call. Probably he should call one of the boys and ask him to go over to Mr. Capper's garage and start folding his papers for him. But which boy? He had only one dime. What if he called Robert's house and Robert's mother answered and said he wasn't home? His dime would be gone.

Henry decided to telephone his own house and ask his mother to call Robert or Murph for him. Once more Henry waited for the traffic signal to change, ran back across the street and into the glass telephone booth in the corner of the service station. He pushed his dime into the smallest hole, dialed, and counted four rings.

"Hello?" It was Mrs. Huggins.

"Say, Mom," began Henry, his eye on the bus stop, "my paper route sort of slipped my mind and I wondered if you would phone Robert or Murph or one of the fellows and ask them to fold my papers for me. I'll get there as soon as I can."

"Henry, where are you?" asked Mrs. Huggins.

"In a filling station out on Lombard Street," answered Henry.

"It is twenty minutes to five now." Mrs. Huggins sounded exasperated. "You'll never get your papers delivered on time."

"Mom, I can't stand here all day arguing,"

Henry pointed out as a bus pulled up to the curb. "Here's my bus now!"

"Honestly, Henry, sometimes I wonder—"

Henry had to cut his mother off.

The traffic signal changed to red just as Henry reached the curb. "Hey, Mr. Bus Driver!" Henry called frantically. The bus driver glanced at him and pulled out into the stream of traffic. He had a schedule to follow and could not wait for one boy. Henry groaned and then he discovered it was not even his bus.

When the signal changed to green Henry walked across the street. He had done all he could do to get his route started and there was no use worrying about it. But Henry did worry. He wondered if his mother was able to find a boy to fold his papers and what Mr. Capper would say when the boy folded Henry's *Journals*. Henry worried when the bus finally came. He worried while he rode on what seemed to be the slowest bus in the world. He worried when he got off and waited for the second bus. He worried when he had transferred to the second bus, which seemed even slower. If there was ever a contest to find the slowest bus in the world, this bus would win. A snail could beat it any day.

And then as the bus finally reached Henry's neighborhood and drove down one of the streets on which Henry should have been delivering papers that very minute, Henry saw a car exactly like the Huggins' car. In fact, it was the Huggins' car. Henry could tell, because he saw his mother get out and throw a folded *Journal* toward a house. She threw awkwardly. The paper did not go far enough so she picked it up and threw again. Henry was horrified. A boy did not want to see his mother delivering papers, especially when she was such a terrible thrower. It was awful. He did not see how anybody could grow up and throw that way.

Hastily Henry jerked the cord that stopped the

bus at the next corner. He bounded out of the door and ran back to Mrs. Huggins, who was consulting his route book to see where to throw the next paper. Henry could not help feeling that he had reached her in the nick of time. He did not want

the passengers on the bus to see her throw again.

"Hey, Mom," he panted. "How come you're delivering my papers?"

"There wasn't anyone else to do it," answered his mother. "I couldn't reach Robert or Murph so I drove over to Mr. Capper's and found the other carriers were leaving with their papers. I've delivered twenty-eight of them."

"Gee, Mom, did you *fold* my papers?" asked Henry. If she had she was better at folding than throwing.

"The other boys had already folded them for you," answered his mother. "They must have known you were going to be late."

Henry opened the car door and pulled out his bag of *Journals*. "I'll take over, Mom," he said, as he slipped the bag over his shoulders. "Thanks a lot. You saved my life."

"You're welcome," answered Mrs. Huggins and then added, "I guess," as she climbed into the car.

Henry had to know something.

Capper say?" he called after his mothe

"He just laughed and wanted to know

taking over your route," answered Mrs. Hugg ns.

Henry wished he had his bicycle. He could actually cover his route almost as fast on foot, but it was more fun to deliver papers on his bicycle. Because he was short for his age the bag of papers bumped against his legs when he went on foot. He walked up one driveway and down the next, remembering which customer wanted his paper left on the doormat and which one had warned him against breaking the geraniums in the flower box on the porch.

Henry walked as fast as he could and soon covered his route. He was late, he knew, but with luck no one would complain—and so far he had been lucky. There was no reason why he should not continue to be. He was tired and sweaty when he reached home, but he was cheerful. The papers were delivered, weren't they? That was all that mattered.

When Henry opened the front door he was surprised to see his father wearing a white shirt and a necktie. Mr. Huggins always wore a sport shirt around home. "Hi, Dad. How come you're all dressed up?" he asked.

"Because your mother had quite a day with one thing or another around here, and we are going to take her out to dinner for a change," said Mr. Huggins.

"Oh—maybe I had better get cleaned up." Henry was surprised at this change in routine. He hoped they would not go to a fancy place with cloth napkins and a long menu. When he went out to dinner he liked to order a hamburger and pie.

"Well, Henry!" Mr. Huggins sounded stern. "Don't you have anything to say for yourself?"

"Why . . . uh . . . I finally got the papers delivered," answered Henry, not quite certain what his father expected of him.

"It seems to me your mother also delivered quite a few papers," said Mr. Huggins.

"Yeah, and golly, Dad, you should see her throw," confided Henry, demonstrating to his father the way his mother delivered papers. "It is pretty awful."

"Henry, I want one thing clearly understood," said Mr. Huggins, ignoring his son's remark. "That paper route is yours. It is not your mother's route and it is not my route. You are to deliver the papers and collect the money and do all the work yourself, and if you can't do it without any help from us, you will have to give the route to someone else. Do you understand?"

Henry looked at the carpet. His father did not often speak to him this way, and he felt terrible. He wanted his father to be proud of him because he was the youngest paper carrier in the neighborhood. "Yes, Dad," he answered. He felt he should offer some explanation for forgetting his route. "I was planning to get some old boards to build a doghouse."

Mr. Huggins grinned. "You don't need to build a doghouse. You're in a doghouse with your mother already."

Mrs. Huggins came clicking into the room on high heels. Henry caught a whiff of perfume and noticed she was wearing one of her best dresses, which meant a restaurant with cloth napkins. She looked so nice Henry felt ashamed of himself for criticizing the way she threw and for wanting a hamburger for dinner. "Gee, Mom, I'm sorry I caused you so much trouble," he said. "It just seemed like such a good chance to go for a ride in a bathtub that I just—well, I forgot all about my route."

"In a bathtub!" exclaimed Mrs. Huggins.

"Sure. Didn't you know? Mr. Grumbie had this old bathtub he was hauling to the dump on a trailer."

"A bathtub! I had no idea—" Mrs. Huggins sat down and began to laugh. "You mean you were riding down Lombard Street in a bathtub?"

"You told me to find something to do," Henry pointed out.

"Yes, I know I did," admitted Mrs. Huggins, "but riding around town in a bathtub wasn't exactly what I had in mind. Honestly, Henry, sometimes I wonder how you get into these things."

"I don't know, Mom, I just do," said Henry thinking with regret of the good idea that had somehow gone wrong. He knew one thing for sure. If he was going to keep his paper route he had better not get into things. He had better keep out of things—especially late in the afternoon.

CHAPTER TWO

Henry and the New Dog

HENRY soon found that there was not enough wood in a bathtub crate to build a really good doghouse. As he rode around the neighborhood delivering papers, he kept his eye out for any old boxes or packing cases that he could use. There was one empty house in the neighborhood which he passed every day hoping he would get some packing cases from the new owners, but the house remained empty. Wood was so scarce that he was about to give up the idea of a house for Ribsy when he had an unexpected piece of luck.

Most of the houses in Henry's neighborhood had been built way back in the nineteen-twenties when cars were shorter and narrower than they are today. Now many people were finding their new cars too long for their old garages and so they built box-like additions onto the ends of their garages to make them long enough for their cars.

One neighbor, Mr. Bingham, was not so fortunate. When he proudly drove his new car into his garage he found there was no way for him to get out of it. His garage was so narrow he could not open the door of his car. So poor Mr. Bingham backed out and parked his car on the driveway. All the neighbors on Klickitat Street had a good laugh over this, and Mr. Bingham announced that he was going to tear down his old garage and build a larger one.

As soon as Mr. Bingham began to tear down the garage, Henry rode his bicycle over to his house to ask if he could have some of the old lumber.

"Sure, Henry, help yourself," said Mr. Bingham, who was prying at a board with a crowbar. "Take all you want but get it out of here before Saturday, when the truck comes to haul it away."

"O.K., Mr. Bingham," agreed Henry. "Do you want to get rid of the windows, too?"

"Take anything you want," said Mr. Bingham.

Doghouse! Why, there would be enough lumber for a clubhouse, a clubhouse with windows and a good one, too. He would save up his paper-route money and buy one of those down-filled sleeping bags he had seen in the window of the sporting goods store and sleep out in the clubhouse he would build out of all the secondhand lumber.

Now Henry found himself with more to do than he had time for. He could not neglect his paper

route, so he saw that he would have to have help. He told his friends Robert and Murph about the free lumber and they saw the point at once.

"Sure, we'll help," they both said. The boys borrowed wagons and every afternoon between school and paper-route time they hauled lumber from Mr. Bingham's driveway to the Huggins' back yard. When Henry left to fold his papers, Robert and Murph went on hauling. By Saturday the boys were sure they had enough lumber for a clubhouse.

"Let's start building," said Henry eagerly.

"Nope," said Murph. "When you build a house, you've got to have a plan. You can't build it any old way."

"Aw, Murph," said Robert. "Where are we going to get a plan?"

Henry, too, was skeptical. He thought that any old way was the only way to build a clubhouse. "Yes, where are we going to get a plan?"

"I can draw one," said Murph. "I'll do it this week end. But remember, when we get the clubhouse built, no girls allowed."

"No girls allowed," vowed Henry and Robert.

"And when we get it built, we can sleep in it in our sleeping bags," added Henry, thinking to himself, when I get a sleeping bag. The boys agreed this was the thing to do with a clubhouse.

Mrs. Huggins looked at the old lumber in her yard and said, "My goodness, Henry, isn't that a lot of lumber?"

"Don't worry, Mom," Henry assured her. "The clubhouse will be real neat when we get it finished and I'll saw up the leftover boards for kindling."

Mr. Huggins looked at the old lumber. "I don't know about this, Henry. It looks to me as if you have taken on a pretty big job."

"The three of us can do it, Dad," said Henry, eager for his father's approval. "And I won't let it interfere with my paper route. Cross my heart."

"See that you don't," said Mr. Huggins. "If you can't handle them both you'll either have to give up your route or tear down the clubhouse."

That week end Murph, who was the smartest boy in the whole school and practically a genius, did draw a plan. He drew it on squared paper, each square equaling one foot. Henry was pretty impressed when he saw it and realized that Murph had been right. It would not do to build a clubhouse any old way.

Murph would not hear of building the clubhouse directly on the ground. "We don't want termites eating our clubhouse," he said.

Henry agreed that it would not do to have bugs chewing away at their clubhouse. This meant the boys had to buy some Kwik-Mix concrete and make four cement blocks for their clubhouse to rest on. It was soon plain to Henry that there was more to building a clubhouse than he had realized and that it was going to take a lot of time—time that he was not sure he had to spare because of his paper route. However, he could not back out now that Robert and Murph had already worked so hard on their new project.

Then one afternoon when Henry was folding his *Journals* on Mr. Capper's driveway with the other paper carriers, Scooter McCarthy spoke. "Say, Mr. Capper, I will be needing one more paper after this," he said.

"Is that so?" Mr. Capper sounded interested. "A new subscriber?"

"That's right, Mr. Capper." Scooter quite plainly was pleased with himself for having sold a subscription.

Henry suddenly pretended to be interested in a headline in the paper he was folding, because he hoped that if he did not look at Mr. Capper, Mr. Capper might not look at him. Henry was ashamed, because it was already October and he had not sold a single *Journal* subscription. Not that he hadn't tried—a little bit. He really had rung several strange doorbells before he became interested in the clubhouse, and had tried to sell subscriptions, but the results were discouraging. Strangers had a way of listening to his sales talk about the *Journal's* easy-to-read type with amused smiles and then saying, "No thank you." One man interrupted with a brusque "Not today" and closed the door in Henry's face. A lady embarrassed him by telling him what a splendid little salesman he was and then saying she couldn't afford to take another paper. Splendid *little* salesman! That was the last straw. After that Henry found it easy to think up excuses for not trying to sell new subscriptions.

Now Mr. Capper was saying, "Good for you, Scooter. Suppose you tell us how you went about selling the subscription."

"Aw, it was easy," boasted Scooter, stuffing his folded papers into his canvas bag. "I just told this man what a good paper the *Journal* was and he said he didn't have time to read it, because he went fishing every Sunday and I said, 'You could use it to wrap your fish eggs in,' and he laughed and said O.K., put him down for a subscription, so I did."

"I call that quick thinking on your part, Scooter," said Mr. Capper. "The rest of the boys could take a lesson from you."

Out of the corner of his eye Henry could see Mr. Capper looking around the group of boys. "What about you, Henry?" asked Mr. Capper. "You haven't turned in any subscriptions since you have had your route."

"Well . . . I—I have been trying," Henry said, admitting to himself that he really had not tried very hard. He had been much too busy with the clubhouse.

"I know it's hard to get started sometimes," said Mr. Capper sympathetically. "I'll tell you what you do. The other day I saw a *Sold* sign on a house on your route. When the new owners move in, you march right up to that front door, ring the doorbell, and sell them a subscription to the paper."

"Yes, sir." Mr. Capper made it sound so easy—march right up and sell them a subscription, just like that. "I'll try, Mr. Capper," said Henry, who knew the house the district manager was referring to. It was the house where he had once hoped to get enough old boxes to build a doghouse. It seemed a long time ago.

And so each day, as Henry delivered his papers, he watched for the new owners to move into the empty house. When he finally did see packing crates and empty cartons stacked on the driveway he decided he should give the people a little time, say about a week, to get settled before he marched right up and rang that doorbell.

The next afternoon Mr. Capper said, "Well, Henry, I see the new owners have moved into the empty house."

"I am going over today as soon as I finish my route," promised Henry, knowing he could not put off the task any longer.

When Henry had delivered his last paper he hung his canvas bag in the garage, washed his hands, combed his hair and, followed by Ribsy, walked the two blocks to call on the new neighbors. He did not ride his bicycle, because it seemed more businesslike to go on foot. Fuller Brush men did not ride bicycles.

As he approached the house he whispered to himself some of the things he planned to say. "Good afternoon. I am Henry Huggins, your *Journal* newsboy. I deliver the *Journal* to a lot of your neighbors." That much he was sure of, but he did not know what to say next. Find a selling point, Mr. Capper always said. Talk about some part of

the paper that would interest a new subscriber.

Henry walked more and more slowly. Ribsy finally had to sit down and wait for him to catch up. The *Journal* had a good sports section . . . a good church section. . . . How was Henry supposed to know what would interest a new subscriber? What if he told someone about the church section when all he wanted was to read the funny papers?

But before Henry could decide what to say, he met Beezus and her little sister Ramona. Ramona was wearing a loop of string around her neck. The ends of the string were fastened with Scotch tape to a cardboard tube.

"Hi," said Henry to Beezus. "What are you doing?"

"Keeping Ramona away from the television set," answered Beezus. "Mother says she spends too much time in front of it."

"Ask me my name," Ramona ordered Henry.

Henry could feel no enthusiasm at all for this new game of Ramona's. "What's your name?" he asked in a bored voice rather than risk Ramona's having a tantrum because he would not play.

Ramona held the paper tube in front of her mouth. "My name is Danny Fitzsimmons," she answered, looking down at the sidewalk and smiling in a self-conscious way that was not at all like Ramona.

"It is not," contradicted Henry. "You aren't even a boy."

"She's just pretending she's being interviewed on the Sheriff Bud program," explained Beezus. "That's her microphone she's holding."

"Oh," was all Henry could find to say.

"My name is Danny Fitzsimmons," repeated Ramona, smiling shyly in an un-Ramona-like way, "and I want to say hello to my mommy and my daddy and my sister Vicki, who is having a birthday, and Mrs. Richards, who is my kindergarten teacher, and Lisa Kelly, who is my best friend, and Gloria Lofton, whose cat just had kittens and she might give me one, and her dog Skipper and all the boys and girls in my kindergarten class and all the boys and girls at Glenwood Primary School and Georgie Bacon's sister Angela, but I won't say hello to Georgie, because I don't like him, and . . ."

"Oh, for Pete's sake." Henry was disgusted with Ramona's new game. "Why don't you just say hello to the whole world and be done with it?" He had no time for this sort of thing. He was on his way to sell a *Journal* subscription and get back to the clubhouse. "So long, Beezus," he said.

". . . and Bobby Brogden who has a loose tooth . . ." Ramona was saying as Henry went on down the street.

When Henry came to the house that was his destination, he turned to Ribsy and said, "Sit," not because he expected Ribsy to sit, but because he wanted to put off ringing that doorbell a little longer. He had not decided what to use as a selling point, because he could not even guess what might interest a new neighbor.

Ribsy sat a moment and then got up and sniffed at the shrubbery.

"I said 'Sit,' " Henry told his dog, deciding that it would be a good idea if Ribsy really did sit. Some people were very particular about dogs running through their flowers and he was anxious to make a good impression.

Like the good dog he was, part of the time, Ribsy sat once more, but he did not stay seated. He stood up and wagged his tail.

"Sit!" ordered Henry sternly, as he started up the steps.

Ribsy appeared to think it over.

"Sit!" Henry raised his voice.

Ribsy waved his tail as if to say, Do I really have to?

A strange dog, a Dalmatian, came trotting around the house and began to investigate Ribsy. The dogs sidled around one another, sniffing. Henry did not pay much attention. Dogs who were strangers to one another always did this.

Next a woman who was wearing an apron, and had a smudge of dust on her cheek, appeared on the driveway at the side of the house. She was older than Henry's mother. Probably she was old enough to be a grandmother. Before Henry had a chance to speak, the Dalmatian left Ribsy and frolicked over to his owner. Ribsy, an agreeable dog who was ready to play, followed.

That was Ribsy's mistake. Now he was trespassing on the Dalmatian's territory. The Dalmatian began to growl deep in his throat and to hold his whiplike tail stiff and straight.

Ribsy stopped short. This was his neighborhood. He was here first. It was the Dalmatian who was trespassing. Each dog began to resent the other's looks, sound, and smell.

"Ribsy!" Henry spoke sharply.

"Ranger!" The woman spoke sharply, too.

The dogs paid no attention to their owners. Each was too intent on letting the other know exactly what he thought of him. The growls grew louder and deeper and they raised their lips and bared their teeth as if they were sneering at each other. And just who do you think you are, Ribsy's growl seemed to say.

I have just as much right here as you have, Ranger's growl answered.

No, you don't, said Ribsy. I was here first.

I'm bigger, growled Ranger.

You're a bully, growled Ribsy.

Get off my property, Ranger told Ribsy.

You make me, Ribsy told Ranger.

"Cut it out, both of you," ordered Henry.

Planning to grab Ribsy's collar and drag him away, Henry jumped down from the steps to the lawn just as the growls erupted into snarls and the dogs went for each other's throat.

"Ranger!" shrieked the woman.

"Ribsy!" shouted Henry. The dogs were on one another in a twisting, tumbling tangle that seemed to be made up of feet, fangs, and tails.

Henry ran over to the snarling, yelping pair and just as he was about to grab Ribsy's collar, he found the other dog's mouth in front of his hand. Quickly he drew back. He saw that he could not stop the fight and since he could not, he wanted Ribsy to win. If it had not been so important for him to sell a *Journal* subscription he would have yelled, "Go get 'im, Ribsy."

"Look out!" shouted the woman. "Don't let him bite you!"

Neighbors began to gather on the sidewalk to watch the excitement. "Dog fight! Dog fight!" a boy yelled.

"The hose!" shouted someone. "Turn the hose on them!"

"I can't," cried the new neighbor. "I don't know where it is!"

"Hey, look at old Ribsy," said Scooter, who had ridden over on his bicycle to see what all the noise was about. "Go get him, Ribsy!"

"You keep quiet!" ordered Henry, even though he wanted to cheer his own dog on.

"Aw, your old mutt couldn't lick a Chihuahua," scoffed Scooter.

"He could, too," said Henry hotly. He wasn't at

all sure Ribsy could lick a Dalmatian, but he could lick a Chihuahua. Henry was positive of that.

"Who's winning?" asked Robert, who had just arrived, along with Beezus and her little sister Ramona.

"The new dog," answered Scooter, and rode on down the street as if the fight was already over.

Half-afraid that Scooter might be right, because the new dog was both bigger and younger than Ribsy, Henry tried once more to reach into the snarling, rolling mass of dog to grab Ribsy's collar. He did not have a chance.

A man grabbed Henry by the arm and pulled him away. "Don't you know that's a foolish thing to do?" he demanded. "Those dogs might bite you."

"Yes, but he's my dog," Henry tried to explain. "I don't want him to get hurt."

The next-door neighbor was screwing the garden hose to the faucet. He turned on the water and advanced toward the dogs with the gushing nozzle in hand. "Stand back, everybody!" he yelled and turned the full force of the hose on the dogs.

Water sprayed in all directions. Still the dogs snarled and snapped. The man with the hose moved closer, so that the force of the hose was stronger. The stream of water caught Ribsy right

in the face and blinded him for the moment. This gave Ranger the advantage. He seized Ribsy by the scruff of the neck, and though Ribsy was a medium-sized dog, Ranger began to shake him. The man turned the hose in Ranger's face.

Ribsy wrenched free and ran dripping down the

street with his tail between his legs, *ki-yi*-ing all the way. The Dalmatian was after him in a flash of black and white.

Henry did not know what to do—whether to run after Ribsy and try to rescue him, or to stay and tell the woman he was sorry his dog got into a fight with her dog, even though it was her dog that started it all. He also wondered what Mr. Capper would think of all this. A fine job of marching right up and ringing that doorbell this had turned out to be.

Before Henry had a chance to decide what to do, Ranger came trotting back down the street looking much pleased with himself. In the next block Ribsy could be heard *ki-yi*-ing toward home.

"Bad dog!" said Ranger's owner, shaking her finger at her pet.

Ranger shook himself with a great clatter of license tags. He did not look one bit sorry. Instead, he looked disapprovingly at Henry, who felt it was wise to retreat to the sidewalk. Ranger walked to the foot of the steps, flopped down, and looked around as if to say, I am monarch of all I survey.

Henry was still trying to collect his thoughts and say something. How had he planned to begin his sales talk? I am Henry Huggins, your *Journal* carrier, but what came next? Ribsy's *ki-yi*-ing in the distance did not help Henry to think.

Before Henry said anything, Ramona passed him and walked right up to Ranger's owner. "Are you the new lady?" asked Ramona.

"Why yes, I am, dear," answered the woman, pleased to have a little girl making friends with her so soon after she had moved into a strange neighborhood.

For once Henry was glad to see Ramona. If she talked to the lady a minute he would have a chance to think of his sales talk once more.

Ramona looked straight at the new neighbor. "Remember," she said with a ferocious frown as

she pointed her finger, "only *you* can prevent forest fires!"

Henry groaned to himself.

The lady looked startled. She had no answer for Ramona.

Beezus ran up to Ramona and grabbed her by the hand. "Don't pay any attention to her," she said apologetically. "She says that to everybody because she hears it on T.V. so much. You know,

Smokey Bear comes on and says it between commercials."

"Oh . . . yes." The lady did not look as if she understood at all. Perhaps she did not own a television set.

"Come on, Ramona." Beezus tugged at her sister's hand.

This was too much. Henry felt the only thing he could do was leave. First his dog got into a fight with the lady's dog and now the little sister of a friend of his practically accused the woman of going around setting forest fires. This was no time to sell a subscription. "I'm sorry about the fight," he blurted and left quickly, followed by Beezus, who was pulling Ramona along by her hand.

"Remember—only *you* can prevent forest fires!" Ramona shouted back to the lady.

That Ramona, thought Henry crossly. She was only five years old but she was the biggest pest in the neighborhood. At the corner Henry paused to glance back. The woman was nowhere in sight but Ranger was sitting on the front porch as if he was standing guard. It seemed to Henry that the dog was challenging him to set foot on his property. Just go ahead and try it, he seemed to say. Go on, I dare you.

To Henry's surprise Mr. Capper did not ask the next day if Henry had sold a newspaper subscription to the new neighbors, and Henry suspected Mr. Capper wanted him to bring up the matter. He didn't see how he could come right out and say, "I didn't get that subscription, because the new neighbor's dog didn't like my dog." Henry made up his mind that since he left Ribsy at home while he delivered papers, he would stop on his route this very afternoon and sell that subscription. By that time Ramona would be home watching television, so she could not spoil his sale a second time.

When all his papers were folded and stuffed

into the canvas bag, Henry mounted his bicycle and zigzagged down the street pitching *Journals* right and left. He was wearing a different T shirt today and he hoped the new lady might have been so busy watching the dog fight that perhaps she hadn't noticed what he looked like. "Good afternoon," he whispered to himself. "I am Henry Huggins, your *Journal* carrier. . . ."

When Henry came to the house he saw Ranger resting on the front porch, his nose on his paws, his eyes watchful. "Hi, Ranger," said Henry, in his most friendly manner.

Ranger's answer was to jump to his feet, barking furiously and leap down the steps after Henry.

There was nothing for Henry to do but pedal down the street as fast as he could go, with the dog snarling and snapping at his right foot every time he pushed down on the pedal. Never had Henry ridden a bicycle so fast. By the time he reached the corner he could no longer breathe in all the air he really needed to keep him going, and each time he bore down on the pedal he expected to lose a piece of his jeans or maybe even a piece of his foot.

By the middle of the next block Ranger suddenly stopped chasing Henry, turned around, and trotted toward home with an air of having done his duty. It seemed to Henry that the dog was not even out of breath.

Henry came to a stop, sat on his bicycle, and panted. Boy! That was close, but the worst of it was that Henry still had to deliver the papers in Ranger's block. When he had caught his breath he parked his bicycle against a tree and returned on foot very, very quietly, being careful to keep out of Ranger's sight. He did not throw the papers. He laid them silently on the lawns and tiptoed away so that he would not disturb Ranger. He had cured Ribsy from running off with newspapers by squirting a water pistol at him every time he went near a paper, but Ribsy was a good-natured dog. Henry did not think he would care to pause long enough to aim at Ranger. He might lose a leg while he aimed. He would like to see Mr. Capper march right up and ring that doorbell. He would have to wear a suit of armor. Or maybe even ride in a tank.

And each time Henry silently laid a paper on a lawn he became a little more angry. He had just as much right around here as that old Ranger. More, because he had lived here longer. And he was a human being, not a dog. By the time Henry had finished delivering the papers in Ranger's block he was just plain mad. He wasn't going to be pushed around by any old dog. No, sir! He was going to get that subscription if it was the last thing he did.

And remembering Ranger's speed and his sharp white teeth, Henry felt that getting that subscription might very well be the last thing he did.

CHAPTER THREE

Trick or Treat

HENRY HUGGINS was sure that this year he had thought up a better Halloween costume than anyone else in his neighborhood. No tramp or clown suit—not for Henry. He had thought up something different, something that no one else would think of in a million years.

There was just one flaw in Henry's anticipation of Halloween. He still had not sold the new neighbor a *Journal* subscription and although Mr. Capper had not mentioned the matter, Henry knew the district manager was waiting for him to say something about it. But what could Henry say? Every time he tried to approach the house Ranger chased him away. How the other *Journal* carriers, especially those in the eighth grade and high school, would laugh at that!

Henry was particularly worried because his father knew Mr. Capper, and if the two men happened to run into each other, Mr. Huggins would probably say, "How's Henry getting along with his route?" and Mr. Capper would answer, "He delivers the papers all right, but he's a terrible salesman." Mr. Capper always said there were three parts to a carrier's job: delivering, collecting, and selling. Then his father would say, "No more work on the clubhouse." He might even tell the boys to tear down the frame which they had so carefully built.

After supper on Halloween Henry tried to shove all this to the back of his mind. It was time to get ready to go trick-or-treating, a time for fun, not a time to think about his troubles. Henry went to his room and shut the door. He got out a bottle of ink (washable, it said on the label and he hoped the label knew what it was talking about) and an old lipstick of his mother's. He went to work and applied war paint to his face. When he finished he did not need a Halloween mask from the dime store like the ones the rest of the boys and girls would wear. No one would guess it was Henry Huggins under the lines and circles he had drawn on his face. Then he fastened an old belt around his head and through it stuck a feather from one of his mother's old hats. Next he draped an Indian blanket around his shoulders and fastened it with safety pins—lots of them. He needed his hands free to carry the paper bag for all the treats he would collect that evening.

Henry studied himself in the mirror and was pleased with what he saw—a fierce Indian that no one would ever guess was really Henry Huggins. But the best part of his costume was still to come. Henry opened his bedroom door. "Here, Ribsy," he called. "Come on, boy!"

Obediently Ribsy trotted down the hall and into Henry's bedroom. Henry opened a bureau drawer and took out a rubber wolf mask which he slipped over Ribsy's head. There! His costume was complete. He was now an Indian accompanied by a wolf, a funny-looking black-and-white-and-brown spotted wolf, it was true, but from the neck up Ribsy was a wolfish-looking wolf with long white fangs and a bright red tongue.

It would certainly be lucky for Henry if he and Ribsy happened to meet Ranger. Boy, old Ranger would take one look at Ribsy-the-wolf and practically turn a backward somersault he would be so surprised and scared. Then he would tuck his tail between his legs and run for home as fast as he could go with Ribsy-the-wolf right after him. By the time Ribsy got through with him, old Ranger would have learned which dog was boss around this neighborhood.

Unfortunately, as was so often the case, this good idea of Henry's had a flaw. With a rubber mask over his head Ribsy would not have a chance

if he got into a dog-fight because he would not be able to bite back. With Ranger he probably would not have a chance *without* a mask. It would be wisest for Henry to stay away from the new neighbor's house that evening. He did not mind. Halloween was no time to sell a newspaper subscription.

Ribsy sat down and scratched.

"Hey, cut that out!" ordered Henry. "You'll tear the mask."

Henry went out to show off his costume to his mother and father. Mr. Huggins laughed and Mrs. Huggins pretended to be frightened at seeing an Indian and a wolf in the house. Nosy, the cat, was really frightened. He fluffed up his tail and jumped to the back of the couch, where he arched his back and kept a wary eye on the wolf.

"Do you think Ribsy is going to stand for that mask very long?" asked Mr. Huggins.

"I think so," said Henry as he opened the front

door. "We've practiced in my room every day this week. When I finished my route I came home and put the mask on him. He seemed sort of puzzled at first, but he's used to it now. I held him up so he could see himself in the mirror, and I think he likes it."

It was a perfect night for Halloween. The stars were bright and a north wind sent leaves skittering along the pavement. Jack-o'-lanterns grinned in front windows. Bands of boys and girls, some of them wearing costumes that glowed in the dark, trooped from door to door. Mothers of small children lurked in the shrubbery, while their little rabbits or ghosts climbed steps and rang doorbells. Henry felt so good he did a war dance in the middle of his front lawn before he started down the street.

Before Henry had had time to ring a doorbell, he met a boy wearing a green cardboard head intended to look like the head of a man from outer space. Suddenly the outer space man's eyes lit up in a fiendish and scary way that made Henry suspect his friend Murph must be inside. Murph was the only boy in the neighborhood who knew enough about electricity to think up such a costume.

Henry raised his hand in an Indian salute. "How," he said, carefully disguising his voice.

Silently the space man held out his hand. Henry grasped it. "Yipe!" he yelled, in his own voice, because he was grasping a buzzer that Murph held in the palm of his hand.

Murph laughed. "I thought it was you under that war paint." He leaned over and patted Ribsy. "Hiya, wolf," he said. "I knew who you were by your spots."

Together the boys proceeded down Klickitat Street ringing doorbells and shouting, "Trick or treat!" Everyone laughed at Ribsy's costume and gave Henry an extra treat for his wolf. Gradually their bags grew fat with candy, peanuts, popcorn balls, individual boxes of raisins, apples, and bubble gum. The boys no longer stopped at every house. They compared notes with other trick-or-treaters and soon learned which people gave jelly beans or all-day suckers. These houses they skipped. They did not like jelly beans and Henry felt that a boy who had a paper route was too grown-up to lick a sucker.

At one house which was completely dark, Henry and Murph hesitated. "Should we bother?" asked Henry. "It doesn't look as if the Morgans are home."

"We might as well skip it," said Murph, and just then a car turned into the driveway and drove into the garage. The headlights revealed a garage cluttered with tools and boxes, and decorated with a collection of old license plates. On a shelf at the back a stuffed owl with wings outstretched and claws poised for attack stared glassily into the night.

"Come on," said Henry, as Mrs. Morgan got out of the car. "She's got a lot of bags in back. Maybe she just bought something good at the market."

The two boys and Ribsy walked up the driveway. "Trick or treat!" shouted Henry and Murph. Murph pressed the button that lit up his outer space head.

"Oh, my goodness!" Mrs. Morgan exclaimed, turning around. "An Indian and a man from space. And a wolf! You certainly startled me." Then she hesitated. "Well . . . I'm afraid you will have to go ahead and play a trick." She peered into the paper bags in the back seat. "I've just come from the market, but all I bought was detergent and coffee and cat food and some things for breakfast. I don't have a thing to treat you with."

This was awkward. Henry could not recall a

Halloween when he had not been treated by everyone. Why, some of the younger children in the neighborhood did not know that trick or treat meant they were supposed to play a trick if they were not given a treat. Neither Henry nor Murph was prepared to play a trick. They had not even brought a piece of soap for soaping windows.

"Aw, that's all right, Mrs. Morgan," said Henry. After all, she was a very nice lady, and one of his *Journal* customers.

"Why, it's Henry Huggins!" exclaimed Mrs. Morgan. "I didn't recognize you in all that war paint."

Naturally Henry was pleased that his neighbor had not penetrated his disguise. "That's a keen owl you have there," he remarked. "It's real fierce-looking, as if it was about to catch an animal or something."

"It's a great horned owl," said Murph, whose

head was full of information like this. "Those license plates go all the way back to 1929."

"Mr. Morgan always nails the old plates on the wall every time he gets a new one." Mrs. Morgan followed Henry's eyes to the owl. "Henry—since I don't have a treat for you, how would you like to have the owl?" she asked, as if she had just had an inspiration.

"Gee, Mrs. Morgan . . ." Henry was almost speechless, he was so busy considering the possibilities of a stuffed owl. In his room on his chest of drawers . . . or in the clubhouse. That was it! In the clubhouse. A stuffed owl was exactly what they needed for a finishing touch. "Gee, could I really have it?"

"Certainly," said Mrs. Morgan. "You boys just climb up on that apple box and lift it down."

The boys quickly obeyed before Mrs. Morgan could change her mind. Henry could scarcely believe his good fortune. The owl was at least five feet from wing tip to wing tip. Why, this was better than all the peanuts and popcorn balls in the world. "Thanks, Mrs. Morgan," said Henry. "Thanks a lot."

"Oh, don't thank me," said Mrs. Morgan. "I've been looking for a way to get rid of that thing for years. It's too big to go into the garbage can, and the Goodwill refused to take it."

"Are you going to put it in the clubhouse?" asked Murph, when the boys had left Mrs. Morgan's garage.

"Sure," said Henry. "Then we can call it a hunting lodge."

"Nobody hunts owls," Murph pointed out.

Henry could see no reason for continuing the rounds of the neighborhood. Nothing he would get could possibly be as good as a stuffed owl. Besides, carrying his paper bag and lugging his owl, which was an awkward size and shape, did not leave him a free hand for ringing doorbells.

On their way home Henry and Murph met a gypsy and a small red devil who turned out to be Beezus and—appropriately, Henry felt—Ramona. They were carrying a jack-o'-lantern that had been carved too long before Halloween. Now its lips were shriveled and there was a smell of cooking pumpkin in the air.

"A stuffed owl!" exclaimed Beezus. "How spooky! What are you going to do with it?"

"Put it in the clubhouse," said Henry, "but no girls are allowed." Henry really would not have minded Beezus' visiting the clubhouse, but Murph had been firm from the beginning. No girls allowed. And perhaps Murph was right. A boy who was in the business of delivering papers was too old to play with girls.

Before Beezus could answer, Ramona held up

her paper bag. "We each got a Nutsie," she said and began to recite. "Nutsies give both children and adults quick energy. Avoid that mid-afternoon slump with a Nutsie, chock-full of protein-rich nuts!"

"Jeepers," said Henry. "What does she do? Memorize commercials?"

"Oh, Ramona," said Beezus impatiently, "stop reciting commercials. You don't have to believe things just because you hear them on T.V." Then she turned to Henry and Murph. "Stay away from that house on the corner," she advised. "When we said, 'Trick or treat' they said they would like to see us do a trick for them and why didn't we sing a little song. I guess they don't understand about Halloween."

"I sang a little song," boasted Ramona, twitching her red devil's tail. "I sang 'Crispy Potato Chips are the best, North or South, East or West, Crispy Chips, hooray, hooray! Get your Crispy Chips today.' "

"And the people thought it was cute," said Beezus crossly. "They asked her to do it again each time."

"It's a nice song," said Ramona. "I like it."

While they were standing under the street light, Scooter McCarthy appeared out of the darkness. He was wearing his father's old Marine uniform, without even a mask, and was licking a candy apple. "Hey, where did you get the owl?" he asked.

"Mrs. Morgan," answered Henry, who suspected Scooter of wanting to let everyone know that his father had been a Marine.

Scooter looked closer. "Sort of beat-up, but not bad," he conceded.

"Where did you get the candy apple?" asked Murph.

"That house where the people moved in last week."

"What are we waiting for?" Murph asked Henry. "Come on, let's get some candy apples."

"Oh . . . I don't know." Henry did not think he cared to meet Ranger when he was wearing an Indian blanket and carrying a stuffed owl. He might trip if he tried to run. There was Ribsy to think of, too. Henry did not want his dog to get in another fight with Ranger.

"Henry is scared of their dog," said Scooter.

"I am not!" said Henry indignantly.

"Then why do you let him chase you every day?" asked Scooter.

Henry wondered how Scooter knew about this. "Come on, Murph, let's go ring the new lady's doorbell." Henry spoke with more assurance than he felt. He only hoped that the dog would feel more friendly toward him when he was not delivering papers and perhaps would not even recognize him in his war paint. Ranger would probably be in the house and, anyway, Henry was not going to be pushed around by a dog. If his owner was giving out candy apples, Henry was going to have a candy apple. If the worst came to the worst he could use the owl to fend off Ranger. He also had the happy thought that it might be pretty hard for Ranger to bite him through the folds of a blanket.

"Sit, Ribsy," Henry ordered, when they were in front of the house. To be on the safe side he pulled off the rubber wolf mask. "Sit!" he said again.

For once Ribsy sat. Probably he was no more eager to meet Ranger than Henry was. As the boys advanced toward the front steps Henry noted that the wind was blowing his scent away from the house. He also thought that since he was disguised with war paint the lady would not recognize him as the boy whose friend had told her that only she could prevent forest fires. That was a good thing. "You ring," he said to Murph, as he rested his bag of treats in front of his feet and held the owl in his left hand. This left his right hand free to accept the candy apple.

Murph turned on his outer-space eyes and rang the doorbell while Henry braced himself. The door opened and the new neighbor, the one to whom Henry was so anxious to sell the *Journal*, appeared.

"Oh!" She clapped her hands to her chest and stepped back, pretending great fright.

"Trick or treat!" shouted Henry and Murph, who could not help being pleased by her performance. Henry was glad that the lady could not possibly recognize him.

Ranger, who was trotting toward the door, saw the owl with its outstretched wings, sharp claws and glittering eyes, looking as if it were about to attack. He skidded to a stop on the hardwood floor, turned, and tried to run, but his claws could not dig into the slippery wood. He slipped and skidded to the edge of the carpet, where his claws could take hold. He slunk under the chair, whimpering with fright.

Old Ranger wasn't so brave after all, Henry thought, as he heard a growl behind him in the

dark. Now that Ranger had turned tail, Ribsy was ready to protect his master.

"Go home!" Henry ordered even though he could not see Ribsy.

The lady bent over and looked under the chair. "What's the matter with Ranger?" she asked. "What's the matter with the boy? Come on out, baby. It's just a stuffed owl. It can't hurt you."

Baby! The lady called that ferocious animal "Baby!" Henry heard the jingle of license tags behind him. He noticed that Ranger had heard them too. Henry wished he had not bothered with a candy apple when he already had a whole bag full of things his mother would not want him to eat.

At that moment Ribsy poked his head around the door.

"Why, it's that dog that got into the fight with Ranger," exclaimed the lady, holding out a tray of candy apples to Henry, "and you must be the paper boy."

Henry accepted an apple. "Uh . . . yes," he admitted now that his disguise had been penetrated. He used his foot to give Ribsy a shove down the steps. "I—I'm sorry about the fight and what Ramona said about not causing forest fires."

"Oh, children and pets!" said the lady, with an airy laugh. "You never can tell what little children are going to say, and I have had a lot of pets and they are always into something. Don't worry about the little girl and please don't worry about Ranger. He'll get over it."

Suddenly a word the woman had spoken repeated itself in Henry's mind. Pets. She was interested in pets! He looked at Ranger whimpering under the chair, steadied his owl, and decided to speak up. Now that the lady knew who he was he had nothing to lose, and somehow he had a feeling it would be easier when he was disguised as an Indian. It was almost as if someone else was speaking instead of Henry. "My name is Henry Huggins," he began. "I am your *Journal* carrier. I deliver the *Journal* to many of your neighbors. The Sunday supplement has a good column about pets you might enjoy reading. . . ." Here he paused to catch his breath, and try to think what to say next.

"Well, it's about time," said the lady with a smile. "I am Mrs. Peabody, and I have been waiting for you to come and sell me a subscription."

"You have?" This possibility had never occurred to Henry.

"Yes, I thought you might want to get credit for selling a subscription," answered Mrs. Peabody.

"Oh, he does," Murph assured her earnestly.

"It took you so long I was about to give up and phone the paper myself," Mrs. Peabody continued.

"Please don't do that," said Henry, lest the lady change her mind about the subscription.

"I won't," Mrs. Peabody assured him. "I have a grown son who used to deliver papers when he was your age and I know all about it."

Henry wondered if she really did know everything about a paper route—things like dogs who chased paper boys. Ranger, it seemed to him, was getting over his scare. He had poked his nose out from under the couch.

"Now don't you worry about my dog," said the lady a second time. "He felt he had to defend his property against intruders, but now that he sees we are friends, he will be all right." She leaned over and spoke to her dog. "Won't you, Ranger, baby?"

Ranger peered out from under the couch and thumped his whiplike tail.

"He's really just a lamb," said Ranger's owner.

Some lamb, thought Henry, but he felt that he should try to make friends with Ranger, so he gave Ribsy another shove with his foot and said, "Hiya, Ranger? How's the fellow?"

Ranger did not growl or bare his teeth. That was progress.

"Well . . . uh . . . thanks a lot for the subscription and the candy apple," said Henry. "I'll start leaving the paper tomorrow."

"Good!" said Mrs. Peabody. "I've missed the crossword puzzle."

She did not say one word about having the paper left in some special place, not a word about being careful not to hit the shrubs or the windows.

Henry could tell this lady was going to be a good customer. Probably she would always be home when he came to collect and would always have the exact change ready.

"Good night, Harry," the lady called after him. She was such a nice lady Henry did not want to tell her his name was Henry, not Harry.

"Well, what do you know," Henry remarked to Murph when they were out on the sidewalk once more. "Two treats—a candy apple and a *Journal* subscription." He felt as if a burden had been taken from him. He had actually sold a subscription, and now that he had sold one, he was sure he could sell others. From now on it would be easy.

Murph laughed. "The way that old Ranger dived under that couch! He sure thought something was after him, but he didn't know what."

Henry laughed too. He laughed at the thought of Ranger skidding on the floor. He laughed because he felt good.

"I've had enough," said Murph. "Let's go home."

"Not yet," said Henry, who no longer felt like going home. "Just one more house."

"What for?" asked Murph. "We have more junk than we can eat now."

"Aw, come on, Murph," coaxed Henry. "Let's stop at Mr. Capper's. I'll bet he's giving something good."

"You just want to tell him about the subscription," said Murph.

"Yup," answered Henry. It was true. News like this could not wait until tomorrow. Now it would be safe for his father to talk to Mr. Capper, who would tell him Henry was a good salesman. There was no danger of his father's telling him to tear down the clubhouse now.

"O.K.," agreed Murph, and the boys started toward Mr. Capper's house with the good news.

CHAPTER FOUR

Henry Collects

THE day after Halloween was the first of November. Henry regretfully had to leave the building of the clubhouse to Robert and Murph, while he called on his subscribers to collect for the *Journal*.

Beezus visited the Huggins' back yard and offered to pound nails in Henry's place. "Ramona is playing over at Lisa's house," she said, "so she won't get in the way."

Murph scowled. "No girls allowed."

"Oh, all right," said Beezus, and flounced down the driveway.

"It won't take me long to collect," said Henry cheerfully, but it was not long before his cheerfulness faded. First of all, he started out to collect without taking any money along. He had to go home and rob his piggy bank so he would have change to give his customers. That took time.

As usual, Henry found that not everyone was home when he rang the doorbell. Sometimes he had to go back a second and even a third time. That took more time. One man who was home had only a twenty-dollar bill. Henry did not have that much change, so he had to make a second trip. And all the time he was eager to get back to the clubhouse.

Henry did have one customer who was just about perfect to collect from. That was Mrs. Peabody. She not only had the exact change ready, she had it waiting on a table by the front door so that Henry was not delayed while she went to get her purse. She also had some cookies wrapped in a paper napkin for him. Ranger behaved himself, too. He watched Henry, but he did not move.

There was only one thing wrong with Mrs. Peabody. She opened the door and said, "Well, here is Harry Higgins to collect for the paper!"

Naturally, since she was such a good customer to collect from, Henry did not like to speak up and say, "Excuse me, my name is Henry Huggins." He just gave her the receipt and thanked her for the cookies.

"You're welcome, Harry," said Mrs. Peabody.

Harry Higgins! Henry wondered how Mrs. Peabody would feel if he started calling her Mrs. Beanbody, not that he intended to. Now that Ranger behaved himself, Mrs. Peabody was his nicest customer, and he would never hurt her feelings.

Then in contrast to Mrs. Peabody there was

Mrs. Kelly, who was Henry's most difficult customer when it came to collecting. The first time Henry walked up the Kellys' walk, which was strewn with tricycles, kiddie cars, and battered kitchen utensils, and rang the doorbell, a little voice inside screamed, "Doorbell, Mommy!"

Mrs. Kelly called from an upstairs window, "Who is it?"

"It's me, Henry Huggins," Henry answered. "I'm collecting for the *Journal.*"

"You'll have to come back some other time," Mrs. Kelly called down. "I'm giving the baby a bath."

The second time Henry rang the doorbell, Mrs. Kelly answered. She wore pedal pushers and an old blouse, and her hair was bound up in a faded scarf. Two small children followed her to the door, and another was crying somewhere in the house. Behind Mrs. Kelly, Henry caught a glimpse of Ramona playing with a little girl her own age.

"Oh, it's you again," said Mrs. Kelly, before Henry had a chance to speak. "I'm sorry. I don't have a cent in the house. You'll have to come back after payday."

Henry realized as he tripped over an old muffin tin on his way down the front steps that he had forgotten to ask Mrs. Kelly when payday was.

Henry was able to drive quite a few nails into the clubhouse before he got up his courage to go back to the Kellys'. The building, under Murph's direction, was going along smoothly when it was not interrupted by Ramona, who was sometimes accompanied by Lisa, her little friend from kindergarten. They wanted to know if they could have nails to take home. They also asked the same riddles over and over.

"How is a dog different from a flea?" Ramona would ask.

"I don't know." Henry was the only boy who bothered to answer.

"Because a dog can have fleas, but a flea can't have dogs," Ramona would answer, and no matter how many times she asked the riddle, she and Lisa screamed with laughter at the answer.

"What is black and white and red all over?" Ramona always asked next.

"No girls allowed!" Murph yelled at this point. Then Ramona and Lisa would walk down the driveway, scuffing the toes of their shoes on the cement to show they were angry. The next day they would be back.

"Can't you find a way to get rid of those pesty girls?" Murph asked.

Henry could only shrug. There was no easy way to get rid of Ramona.

Finally Henry decided he had to get up his courage to go back to the Kellys', or Mr. Capper would start asking him why he had not finished collecting.

This time Mrs. Kelly met him at the door with a baby balanced on her hip. "Oh, it's you again," she said for a second time, glancing over her shoulder toward the kitchen, where Henry could hear an automatic washing machine running. "Come in while I find my purse."

Henry stepped into the living room, which was scattered with toys, children's clothing, and crumpled pages torn from magazines. There was a bowl of soggy breakfast food on the coffee table.

A little boy who was sucking his thumb and holding an egg beater looked out of the kitchen door.

"Don't pinch your fingers in the egg beater, Kermit," said Mrs. Kelly. She looked wearily at Henry. "Would you mind keeping an eye on the children while I go find my purse? They are all in the kitchen. Kermit, Bobby, Lisa, and her little friend."

"Sure." What else could Henry say? Anything to collect and get back to his clubhouse. He stepped into the kitchen where the washing machine was busily swish-swashing. Lisa and her little friend, who turned out to be Ramona, were kneeling on chairs at the kitchen table, cutting circles out of Play-Doh with cookie cutters.

"I know him," said Ramona to Kermit and Bobby. "That's Henry Huggins."

"Let's cross him out," suggested Lisa. Laughing wildly, the two little girls made big crisscross motions in the air in front of Henry.

"There," said Ramona. "I guess we crossed him out."

Henry did not know what to make of this and did not have time to give the matter much thought, because Bobby started to crawl out of the kitchen. Henry did not know how old Bobby was, but he knew he couldn't be very old, because he was wearing diapers, plastic pants, and a T shirt. In one hand he carried a piece of toast. Henry had never seen a baby drool as much as Bobby. As he crawled he left little puddles on the floor.

Henry heard Mrs. Kelly's footsteps going up the stairs. Bobby dropped his toast on the floor. Lisa and Ramona giggled over some private girl joke. Kermit spun the egg beater and made a noise like machinery with his mouth. The washing machine churned. A dog walked into the kitchen, picked up Bobby's toast, and dropped it again. It did not look as if anyone would get into trouble, but just the same Henry hoped their mother would hurry back. He was a paper carrier, not a baby sitter.

Bobby picked up the soggy toast the dog had dropped and began to chew it. "Hey," said Henry feebly. He was pretty sure babies were not supposed to eat toast that had been in a dog's mouth. Gently he tried to take the toast from Bob, who clung to his crust and uttered a piercing scream. Henry backed away. Bobby put the toast back in his mouth and gnawed contentedly. Oh well, thought Henry, it looks like a pretty clean dog.

Then Henry discovered Kermit was missing. He stepped into the living room where Kermit was twirling the egg beater in time to see the dog lap up the soggy breakfast food in the bowl on the coffee table. "Cut that out," said Henry even though it was too late to do any good.

The washing machine stopped swish-swashing and was silent as if it was resting up before starting to spin.

Mrs. Kelly called down from upstairs, "Kermit, what did you do with my purse?"

"I put it under the bed so Bobby wouldn't get it," answered Kermit.

Henry heard a chair being dragged across the kitchen floor. Followed by Kermit and the dog he went back to investigate. Ramona was standing on a chair in front of the washing machine. She was not actually doing anything wrong, but knowing her, Henry was not taking any chances. "You better get down from there," he said.

"Pooh," said Ramona.

The washing machine gave a loud click and started to spin. Ramona reached toward the lid.

"What do you think you're doing?" Henry spoke more forcefully this time.

"I don't have to mind you," Ramona informed him. "You're just an old boy." She lifted the lid of the washing machine to peek inside. Instantly dirty water and detergent spun out of the machine with a great *whoosh*, hitting Henry right in the face, drenching Ramona and spraying the whole kitchen.

"Cut that out!" yelled Henry, snatching Ramona off the chair and slamming down the lid of the washing machine, but not until the jet of dirty water had circled the kitchen several more times.

All the children were howling with fright and Ramona howled the loudest. The dog shook himself and began to bark. Henry mopped his face with his damp sleeve and looked around at the rivulets of dirty water trickling down the walls and cupboard doors onto the floor. It was a wet, sloppy mess, and there was no time to clean it up. "What did you have to go do that for?" he demanded of Ramona, as Mrs. Kelly's feet came thumping down the stairs.

Ramona who was dripping with dirty water

stopped howling and looked sulky. "I just wanted to see what it looked like inside when it was spinning," she said.

Disgusted as he was, Henry felt a small flash, a very small flash, of understanding for Ramona. He had always been curious to see a load of spinning clothes, too.

"Oh, my goodness!" exclaimed Mrs. Kelly from the doorway as she looked at the wet children and dripping walls. The children's howls subsided when they saw their mother. "What on earth happened?"

"I'm awfully sorry," Henry apologized. "I tried to stop Ramona, but she lifted the lid of the washing machine before I could get to her." He glared at Ramona, who made a face right back at him.

"Tattletale," said Ramona.

Maybe he was a tattletale, but Henry didn't know what else he could have told Mrs. Kelly. She would know the washing machine did not open itself. "I'll help wipe it up," he offered, feeling this was the least he could do.

Mrs. Kelly looked around her dripping kitchen. "Oh well," she said with a sigh. "I suppose I should wash down the walls sometime. No, don't bother to help. You just take Ramona home so she can get cleaned up and into some dry clothes."

"O.K. . . ." Henry tried to sound willing. "I'm sure sorry, Mrs. Kelly. I'd be glad to come back and help clean up."

Mrs. Kelly managed a smile. "No thank you, Henry. You've done enough already."

Henry was not at all sure how she meant this remark. "Come on, Ramona," he said, anxious to get away.

Outside, Ramona pushed her wet hair back from her forehead so it wouldn't drip into her eyes and said, "I can go home by my own self."

"That's all right with me," said Henry crossly.

He knew that now that Ramona went to kindergarten, she was allowed to cross all but the busiest streets alone.

Ramona went her way and Henry went his. When he came to Klickitat Street he found Mrs. Peabody out raking up leaves from her lawn. Ranger, who was lying on the porch, looked suspiciously at Henry, but did not move.

"Why, Harry Higgins!" she exclaimed. "You're all wet."

"Yeah, I know," said Henry sheepishly. He was trying to find a polite way to let Mrs. Peabody know his name was not Harry Higgins. Then his thoughts began to leap. Mrs. Peabody. His paper route. The money for the *Journal.* He had forgotten to get the money from Mrs. Kelly!

Henry's thoughts were in a turmoil as he walked down the street. He could not go back and ask Mrs. Kelly for the money after what had happened. He would just skip the whole thing and pay for the Kellys' papers himself. Nobody would ever know the difference. No, he wouldn't either. He would never save enough for a sleeping bag if he did that. Yes, he would, too. He could never, never bring himself to ring that doorbell again. Yes, he could. No, he could not. That Ramona! She was the cause of all this. A little old kindergartner.

That settled the matter for Henry. He was not going to let a girl in kindergarten keep him from getting the money he had coming to him. Henry turned around and started back toward the Kellys' house.

"Well, Harry, did you forget something?" asked Mrs. Peabody.

"Yes, I did," answered Henry, managing to sound polite. He was so disgusted with Ramona that he felt like snapping at the whole world. First she had told Mrs. Peabody only she could prevent forest fires, and now this. If she ever caused him any more trouble on his paper route he would . . .

he would . . . do something. What he would do he did not know.

Henry marched straight up the steps and rang the Kellys' doorbell.

Lisa looked out of the window smeared with little fingerprints and screamed, "Mommy, it's that boy again!"

When the door opened, Henry was the first to speak. "Mrs. Kelly, I am sorry to bother you again, but I didn't get the money for the paper when I was here before." He was still so disgusted with Ramona he forgot to be embarrassed.

"I thought you would be back." Mrs. Kelly laid down the cellulose sponge in her hand and picked up her purse, which was lying on a chair near the door.

Henry accepted the money and gave Mrs. Kelly a receipt. Whew, he thought, I hope I never have to go through this again. And he decided he had better make sure that he did not. "Uh . . . Mrs.

Kelly," he ventured, "what day would be best for me to collect?"

"The first Saturday of the month," answered Mrs. Kelly. "That is payday."

Henry pulled his route book out of his hip pocket and made a note after the Kellys' name. "Collect 1st Sat." There. That ought to show Mrs. Kelly he could be businesslike. "Thank you," he said, and once more started for home. Now he did not care if he was damp and dirty. He had actually collected from every single one of the forty-three customers on his route. The job was finished until the first of next month and now he could go back to working on the clubhouse.

"Did you get what you went after, Harry?" asked Mrs. Peabody as Henry passed her house for the third time that afternoon.

"I sure did." Henry was now feeling so confident that he was certain someday he would be able to find a way to let Mrs. Peabody know his name was not Harry Higgins. He would even find a way to keep Ramona from causing him trouble on his route. He would find a way to keep her away from the clubhouse, too.

Henry realized that it was now too late for him to do any work on the clubhouse this afternoon. Tomorrow afternoon the first thing he would do was make a sign saying, "No girls allowed."

The only thing wrong with this idea was that Ramona could not read.

CHAPTER FIVE

Ramona and the Clubhouse

WHENEVER it was not raining, Henry and his friends worked hard on the clubhouse. They measured and sawed and nailed, according to Murph's plan. When Henry was delivering his papers he noticed that one of his customers was having his roof covered with asphalt shingles, and he was able to persuade the workmen to give him enough leftover material to shingle the roof of the clubhouse. He bought two big hinges, so they could have a door that would really open and close.

Beezus and Ramona and sometimes Lisa came over almost every day to watch the progress of the building. They stayed until time for the Sheriff Bud program on television, which Ramona never missed.

"I could help," offered Beezus. "I bet I can drive nails."

"No girls allowed," said Murph curtly.

"I could make curtains for the windows," suggested Beezus.

"Who wants curtains?" answered Henry, who would have been willing to let Beezus help, because for a girl she was pretty sensible, but when a boy is working with other boys he sometimes feels he has to act the way they do.

So Beezus sat on the Huggins' back steps and watched, while Ramona amused herself. Ramona never had any trouble keeping herself entertained. She climbed to the top step and began to count, "Ten, nine, eight, seven, six, five, four, three, two, one. *Blast off!*" Then she jumped to the ground.

"I know where I could get an old door mat," suggested Beezus hopefully.

"What's the use of having a clubhouse if you have to wipe your feet like in a regular house?" asked Robert.

It was not possible for Beezus to make a suggestion that would please the boys. "Get lost," said Murph rudely.

"Well, all right for you, smarty!" It was easy to see that Beezus' feelings were hurt. "Mess around with your old boy stuff. See if I care! Come on, Ramona, let's go home. It's almost time for Sheriff Bud."

Ramona finished blasting off and trotted along home with her sister.

Henry was really sorry to see Beezus' feelings hurt, but he did not like to say so in front of the other boys, who were too busy installing the real glass windows to pay any attention to what had just happened.

While the boys worked, Murph began to recite some strange sounds. They were not words, so Henry and Robert had trouble catching exactly what it was he was saying. The syllables, whatever they were, had a catchy sound and rhythm.

"Say that again, Murph." Henry found himself wanting to make the sounds himself.

Once more Murph rattled off the syllables. This time Henry caught a "beep" and a "boom."

"Hey, that sounds keen," said Robert. "Where did you learn that?"

"From my cousin in California," answered Murph. "He learned it from a lifeguard."

"Say it again and slow down," said Henry. "I want to learn it."

Murph laid down his hammer and recited slowly and distinctly.

"Fadatta, fadatta, fadatta,
Beepum, boopum, bah!
Ratta datta boom sh-h
Ahfah deedee bobo."

Henry and Robert laid down their tools, too. "Fadatta . . . fadatta . . . fadatta." They began slowly at first but in a few minutes they had mastered the sounds and could rattle them off as fast as Murph.

"Hey, I have an idea!" Henry was enthusiastic. "We could be a club and use it for our secret password and always say it so fast other kids couldn't learn it."

"Sure," agreed Robert. "All the kids will want to learn it and we won't teach it to them."

"Especially girls." Murph picked up a screw driver and went to work to install the door hinges.

At last the clubhouse was finished. The siding was snug and tight. The hinges worked perfectly, the asphalt shingles were nailed down so securely the roof could not possibly leak. Yes, the boys agreed, it was a good solid house. It was just about as solid as a real house. They thumped the walls appreciatively and stamped their feet on the floor.

And the best part of it was, it was big enough for three boys to sleep in if they didn't move around much, and who could move around in a sleeping bag?

"Yes, sir, solid as the rock of Gibraltar." Murph spoke with pride, for he was the one who had drawn up the plans in the first place.

Then Murph built a shelf and Henry went into the basement and lugged out the stuffed owl which his mother would not let him keep in his room, because she thought it looked as if it had moths. He set the owl on the shelf. It was exactly what the place needed, a really masculine touch.

"Fadatta, fadatta, fadatta," chanted the boys.

"When we all get sleeping bags we can spend the night out here," said Henry.

Robert and Murph, it developed, already had sleeping bags, so Henry dropped the subject. He did not want them sleeping in the clubhouse while he slept in his own bed. Fortunately it was time for him to start his paper route, so there was no more discussion of sleeping in the clubhouse.

Then mysterious things began to happen in the clubhouse. One day after school Henry found the owl's glass eyes turned so that it looked cross-eyed. That's funny, he thought. He straightened the eyes and forgot about them.

But the next day when Henry and Robert entered their clubhouse they were startled to see that the owl, its eyes once again crossed, appeared to be smoking a cigarette. Upon closer examination they found that a small tube of white paper had been fastened to the owl's beak with Scotch tape.

"How do you like that!" Robert ripped off the cigarette in disgust while Henry straightened the eyes once more. "I'll bet old Beezus did this."

That was just what Henry was thinking. He felt

a little disappointed that sensible Beezus would do a thing like this, not that he could really blame her after the way she had been treated. . . .

The boys found a can of paint in Henry's garage and started painting a *No Girls Allowed—This Means You,"* sign, which Robert finished after Henry went to start his paper route.

The next afternoon Henry, Robert, and Murph raced home from school on their bicycles to protect their clubhouse from a possible invasion of Beezus and Ramona. When they opened the door they found the owl's eyes were crossed once more, it was wearing a doll's pink bonnet with a ribbon tied under its chin—if an owl could be said to have a chin—and in its beak it held a crayoned sign that said: *Down with boys!*

"Well, how do you like that!" exclaimed Henry, thinking that Beezus must have come in the morning before school, because they had ridden so fast she could not possibly have reached the clubhouse ahead of them this afternoon.

"The nerve of some people," said Robert. "A doll bonnet on our owl!"

"That's a girl for you." Murph tore down the sign.

"A lock, that's what we need," said Henry.

"A padlock," agreed Murph.

"With a key," said Robert.

Henry dug into his pocket for some of the money he had earned on his route, and the three boys rode off to the hardware store to select a clasp and padlock. When they returned, the owl was holding a sign that said: *Ha ha, you think you are smart.*

Murph screwed the clasp in place, because he was the fastest with tools. While he worked, Henry and Robert decided that because the lock came with only two keys and each member could not have one, they should find two secret hiding places. They talked it over in whispers and after looking around to make sure Beezus was not hiding in the shrubbery, they hid one key under an oilcan in the garage and the other under a flowerpot on the back porch. They vowed always to put the keys back in place, because it would not be fair for any one boy to carry a key when there were not enough keys to go around.

It was with a feeling of a deed well done that the boys snapped shut the padlock when it was time for Henry to start his route. That would keep old Beezus out! She could not possibly get in now. The house was solidly built and the windows taken from the old garage were not the kind that could be opened.

After that the boys had no more trouble. Their next project was painting the house. The front and the north side were to be white, while the back and the south side were to be green. The boys did not have enough paint of one color for the whole house, and anyway, as Murph pointed out, nobody could see all four sides at the same time. Henry painted a little each afternoon before starting his route, and Robert and Murph continued to work after he had gone.

Beezus and Ramona sometimes walked up the driveway to see what was going on. When the boys ignored them, they went away, but they did not go away quietly, because Ramona was always singing some tune or other that she had learned from television. Sometimes it was a song about shampoo, but usually it was a verse about a bread that builds strong bodies eight different ways.

"I guess we fixed her," the boys congratulated one another. "You won't catch her bothering us any more." And when the girls were gone they chanted their magic words:

"Fadatta, fadatta, fadatta,
Beepum, boopum, bah!
Ratta datta boom sh-h
Ahfah deedee bobo."

All for one and one for all. That was Henry, Robert, and Murph.

Then one cold November afternoon Henry came home from school to find that his mother had left a note telling him she had gone downtown and would not be back until six o'clock. She also told him not to eat any pie. Henry used his finger to wipe up some juice that had oozed through the piecrust. *M-m-m.* Blackberry. Then he made himself a peanut-butter sandwich and with Ribsy trotting after him, went outside, where he removed a key from under the flowerpot, unlocked the clubhouse, and carefully returned the key to its hiding place.

Henry stepped inside the clubhouse and patted

the owl's head. Everything was in order. Ribsy curled up in a corner and prepared to go to sleep.

"Hello." It was Ramona's voice.

Henry turned and saw the little girl sitting on the back steps. She was bundled up, because the day was cold and she too was eating a peanut-butter sandwich.

"Oh . . . hello," he said. "Where's Beezus?"

"Home."

"Why didn't she come with you?" Henry felt that Ramona could cause enough trouble when she was with Beezus. He did not want her around without her older sister to look after her.

"Because you are mean to her," answered Ramona.

Henry felt slightly uncomfortable, because there was truth in what Ramona said. Even so, boys had a right to do boy things without girls around, didn't they? And Beezus didn't have to mess up their clubhouse, did she?

He looked at Ramona sitting on the steps chewing her peanut-butter sandwich. "Why don't you go home?" he asked, seeing no reason for being hospitable to Ramona.

"I don't want to," said Ramona, and went on chewing.

Well, as long as she had a sandwich to keep her busy . . . Henry looked around the clubhouse to see how it could be furnished. An orange crate nailed to the wall would make a good cupboard. He measured the space with his hands. Yes, an orange crate would be just the right size.

Henry was aware that the clubhouse had suddenly grown darker. He turned and saw that the door must have blown shut. Just then he heard a *snap* and he had a terrible feeling. He tried the door. It was locked. Locked from the outside and there was only one person who could have done it—Ramona.

Henry looked out of the window and saw

Ramona sitting on the steps, calmly licking her fingers. "You let me out of here!" he yelled.

Ramona stopped licking long enough to answer. "I don't have a key."

This stopped Henry. Of course she did not have a key. Both keys were carefully hidden and he was not going to tell any girl where they were, either. He could get out some way.

Henry threw his shoulder against the door. Nothing happened. It was a good, solid door. He threw his shoulder against the walls. Still nothing happened. They were good solid walls. Henry rubbed his shoulder and decided that Murph had done a good job of planning the clubhouse. Maybe too good.

Next he jumped up and down as hard as he could. The floor was a good solid floor. The whole clubhouse, Henry concluded, was as solidly built as a jail, and right now that was exactly what it was.

Next Henry considered breaking a window. He looked around, but there was not a hammer or a stick of wood he could use. If he slammed his fist through the glass, he would be sure to cut himself, and even if he did break the glass, the windows were divided into four small panes and he had no way of removing the dividing pieces of wood.

Next Henry tried yelling. "Help! Help!" he shouted at the top of his voice. "Help! Help!" Ribsy stood up and barked. Nothing happened. Nothing at all unless you counted the pleased look on Ramona's face. Where was everybody anyway?

"Huh-huh-huh-help," said Ramona, as if she were thinking very hard. Little puffs of vapor came out of her mouth, because the afternoon was so cold. "Help begins with an *h!*" Plainly Ramona was pleased with herself for making this discovery. Her kindergarten teacher was teaching her class the sounds the letters make.

Henry knew that his mother was downtown.

Robert was getting a haircut, Beezus was home, and he did not know where Murph was. Then he caught a glimpse of Mrs. Grumbie, his next-door neighbor looking out of an upstairs window. "Help!" he yelled, pounding on the door. "Let me out!"

Mrs. Grumbie nodded and waved. She was used to boys playing in Henry's back yard.

There was nothing to do, Henry decided, but try to make himself comfortable until his mother came home. He sat down on the floor and leaned against the wall. Ho-hum. It was going to be a long, cold wait. He felt cross and disgusted. That Ramona . . . that pest . . .

Suddenly Henry leaped to his feet. His route! His paper route. He *had* to get out. He could not stay trapped until six o'clock or he wouldn't get his papers delivered in time. And he knew what his father would say about that. Boy!

The only thing to do, Henry decided, was to tell

Ramona where the key was and to get her to unlock the padlock. That would not be so terrible, now that he stopped to think about it. All he would have to do was find another hiding place after Ramona had gone home.

Henry looked out of the window. Ramona was no longer on the steps. Apparently she had lost interest in Henry when he was silent, because now she was skipping down the driveway. He couldn't let her go. She was his only hope.

"Ramona! Wait!" yelled Henry.

Ramona stopped and looked back.

"Come here," called Henry. "I want to tell you something."

This tempted Ramona. She walked back and stood under the clubhouse window, looking up at Henry.

Henry had a feeling that if he was going to get Ramona to do what he wanted he had better make this good. "Uh . . . Ramona, I am going to let you in on a secret. A big secret."

Ramona, who liked secrets, looked interested.

Henry decided to build it up. "A secret that only *boys* know," he added impressively.

"I don't like boys," Ramona informed him. "Boys are mean."

Henry saw that he had better choose his words with more care. At the same time he had to hurry, because it was almost time to start his route. "Only three people in the whole world know the secret." He watched Ramona's reaction. She seemed to be waiting for him to go on.

Henry lowered his voice as much as he could and still make himself heard through the glass. "I am going to tell you where the key to the clubhouse is—"

"Where?" demanded Ramona.

"Wait a minute," said Henry. "First you have to

promise something." He worked hard to look as if there was something mysterious and exciting about the promise he was about to extract, but it was hard work. He was tired of the game and wanted to get out. Now. "If you promise to unlock the padlock, I will tell you where the key is."

Ramona stared stonily at Henry. "I don't want to."

"But *why?*" Henry was desperate.

"I just don't," Ramona informed him.

Oh-h. Henry groaned. Then he was mad, just plain mad. That Ramona! She was going to make him lose his route, and then he would never get his sleeping bag, and his father would be cross with him, and Mr. Capper would find a bigger boy to take the route. . . . Henry banged his fist against the side of the clubhouse. For some reason that made him feel better. He began to stamp his feet and pound his fists and yell. At least, he thought grimly, this was keeping Ramona interested. And he couldn't let her get away. She was his only hope . . . almost, it seemed, his only contact with civilization. It occurred to him that it must be almost time for the Sheriff Bud program on television, and Ramona never missed Sheriff Bud.

It seemed silly to yell "help!" and "let me out!" when nobody was going to help him or let him out. Henry tried a Tarzan yell. Ramona sat down on the back steps and propped her chin up on her fist.

"Open Sesame!" yelled Henry, just in case it might work. The door remained shut.

Then in desperation Henry tried the club yell, hoping that somehow it would work like a magic spell.

"Fadatta, fadatta, fadatta,
Beepum, boopum, bah!
Ratta datta boom sh-h
Ahfah deedee bobo!"

To his surprise it did work like a magic spell. Ramona got up and came over to the clubhouse window. "Say that again, Henry," she begged.

This time it was Henry's turn to say no. To do so gave him great satisfaction.

"Please, Henry."

Henry saw that he had a bargaining point. A girl who would sing television commercials would naturally like something that sounded really good. "I'll say it again if you get the key and unlock the padlock first."

Ramona thought it over. "Puh-puh-puh-padlock begins with a *p!*" she said triumphantly.

Henry groaned. "I *know* padlock begins with a *p*," he said. "Now will you get the key?" Then he added hastily. "Key begins with a *k*."

"We haven't had *k* yet at school." Ramona seemed suddenly agreeable. "Where is the key?" she asked.

Feeling like a traitor to Robert and Murph,

Henry revealed the secret. "Under the flowerpot on the back porch."

Ramona found the key and Henry could hear her fumbling as she inserted it in the padlock. "Say it," she ordered.

Henry rattled off the club's secret words. "Now unlock it," he begged, and outside he could hear Ramona struggling with the padlock.

"I can't," she said. "I can't make the key turn."

Henry pressed his nose against the window. "Look," he said, "go get Beezus. If you do, I'll teach you both to say fadatta, fadatta, fadatta. And . . . tell her I'm sorry."

I am a traitor, thought Henry, a one-hundred-per-cent traitor. But what else could he do? He had to get his papers delivered somehow. Then he began to worry about Ramona. Maybe she would forget to tell Beezus. Maybe she would remember Sheriff Bud, turn on the television set, and forget all about him.

There was nothing Henry could do but wait. Actually he did not wait very long, but it seemed that way. It seemed to him that he waited and waited and waited. The clubhouse felt colder and damper and more like a dungeon every minute.

At last Henry heard footsteps coming up the driveway. Beezus had come to his rescue—he hoped. Beezus was alone, and Henry guessed that Ramona had stayed home to watch television. "Hi, Beezus," he called through the window. "It's sure nice of you to come and let me out . . . after the way I have . . . uh . . . acted." The last words Henry found difficult to speak, but he felt better when he had said them.

Beezus looked as if she had not made up her mind to let Henry out. "I didn't say I was going to let you out," she reminded him. "You don't want girls around, you know."

Henry had no answer for this. "Aw, come on, Beezus," he pleaded. "I've got to start my route."

Beezus thought it over. "All right, I'll let you out, but only because I know you have to start your route," she agreed, like the sensible girl she was. "But first teach me the secret words."

Henry knew when he was licked. "Oh, all right, if that's the way you feel about it. Fadatta . . . fadatta . . . fadatta."

"Fadatta . . . fadatta . . . fadatta," Beezus repeated gravely.

"Beepum, boopum, bah."

"Beepum, boopum, bah." Fortunately Beezus learned quickly and soon mastered the secret words. She was a girl who kept her part of the bargain. She unlocked the padlock and slipped it out of the clasp. "There," she said.

"Thanks, Beezus," said Henry, as he stepped out to fresh air and freedom. He picked up his bicycle. He had no time to talk if he was going to get his papers folded and delivered.

Beezus did not seem to mind that Henry was in

such a hurry. "Fadatta, fadatta, fadatta," she chanted. "Good-by, Henry. I'm going home to teach the secret words to Ramona like I promised."

Henry threw his leg over his bicycle and pedaled down the driveway. Now the secret words would be all over the neighborhood. Robert and Murph would not like it, but Henry hoped that since they knew Ramona they would understand and not mind too much.

That Ramona! thought Henry. Always causing him trouble on his route. He would have to do something about her, but what anybody could do about Ramona, he did not know. All he knew was that if he was going to keep his paper route and his clubhouse he had better do something, and do it soon.

CHAPTER SIX

Henry Writes a Letter

NATURALLY as soon as Ramona learned the secret words, she recited them every chance she got and soon they were all over the neighborhood. They were all over Glenwood School, too. Everywhere Henry went he heard fadattas and beepum, boopum, bahs. He began to wish he had never heard the silly thing. Quite a few mothers felt this way, too, and asked their children *please* to stop saying that—that *thing*. But the whole school went right on saying fadatta, fadatta, fadatta.

And all because of Ramona. Yes, Henry decided, something was going to have to be done about Ramona, but what he did not know.

"Say, Mom," Henry said one evening, "how can I keep Ramona from being such an awful pest all the time?"

"Just don't pay any attention to her," answered Mrs. Huggins.

"But Mom," protested Henry. "You don't know Ramona."

Mrs. Huggins laughed. "Yes, I do. She is just a lively little girl who gets into mischief sometimes. Ignore her, and she will stop bothering you. She only wants attention."

Henry could not help feeling that his mother did not understand the situation. He had ignored Ramona. That was the whole trouble. He was not paying any attention to her so he had found himself locked in the clubhouse. This was not a little mischief. It was a terrible thing for her to do.

"Surely you are smarter than a five-year-old," remarked Mr. Huggins jokingly.

Henry did not have an answer for his father, who, after all, was safe in his office all day and did not know what a nuisance Ramona could be.

Next Henry consulted Beezus. "Ramona sure causes me a lot of trouble on my route," he remarked one afternoon. "Isn't there some way to get her to stop pestering me?"

Beezus sighed. "I know. I've told Mother, and Mother has told her to behave herself, but you know how Ramona is. She never listens."

"I know," Henry said gloomily. Ramona was a real problem. When Mrs. Quimby persuaded her to stop doing one annoying thing, Ramona promptly thought up something entirely new but equally annoying. If only Henry could find a way to stay ahead of Ramona. . . .

One afternoon Henry arrived at Mr. Capper's garage in plenty of time to fold his papers. He counted his stack of forty-three *Journals* and as long as he was early, he took time to glance through the paper. He looked at the headlines and read the comic section. Then a picture of a smiling lady caught his eye. It was the lady who gave people advice when they wrote to her about their problems.

Because he had a problem, Henry paused to read her column. A girl who signed her letter, "Flat Broke" said that her father did not give her a big enough allowance. Her father did not understand that she needed more money for school lunches, bus fare, and other things. What should she do about it? The smiling lady told her to talk it over with her father and explain to him exactly what her expenses were. The smiling lady was sure he would understand.

Henry thought this over. Maybe he should write

to the lady about Ramona. He could write, I have a problem. A girl in my neighborhood has a little sister who pesters me on my paper route. How can I get her to stop? Then he could sign the letter Disgusted.

Henry tried to think how the lady would answer his letter. Dear Disgusted, she would say, but what would she say next? Probably she would tell him to talk his problem over with Ramona's mother and everything would be all right. Oh no, it wouldn't, thought Henry, just as if he had really read an answer to a letter he had really written. Ramona's mother knew all about his problem and had not been able to solve it. As Beezus said, Ramona never listened very much.

Henry began to fold his papers. There must be somebody Ramona would listen to. And then a picture in an advertisement gave Henry an idea. Santa Claus! Ramona might listen to Santa Claus. Henry grinned to himself. He would really fix

Ramona if he waited until Christmas Eve and climbed up on the Quimbys' roof and yelled down the chimney in a deep bass voice, Ho-ho-ho, Ramona Geraldine Quimby, you stop pestering Henry Huggins on his paper route or I won't leave you any presents. Ho-ho-ho.

"Ho-ho-ho," said Henry out loud, to see how much like Santa Claus he could sound.

Just then Mr. Capper came out of the back door. "Who do you think you are? Santa Claus?" he asked.

"No, sir." Embarrassed, Henry went on folding papers.

Still, Henry was pleased with this picture of himself ho-ho-hoing down the chimney at Ramona, but unfortunately there was just one thing wrong with it. Boys were not allowed to go climbing around on their neighbors' roofs on Christmas Eve or any other time. And anyway, Ramona

might not even listen to Santa Claus. Henry would not be at all surprised.

Henry was zigzagging down the street on his bicycle, throwing papers to the right and to the left, when he saw Beezus and Ramona hurrying along the sidewalk. Ramona was wearing a mustache cut from brown paper and stuck to her upper lip with Scotch tape. Henry recognized this as another attempt to copy one of Sheriff Bud's disguises.

"Hi, Beezus," he said.

Ramona pulled at Beezus' hand. "Come on," she said. "Come on, or we'll be late."

"I can't understand it," remarked Beezus. "She can't even tell time, but she always knows when it's time for the Sheriff Bud program."

"Like Ribsy," said Henry. "He can't tell time either, but he always knows when it's time to meet me after school." He pedaled on down the street, when suddenly a thought struck him. *Sheriff Bud.* If there was anyone Ramona would listen to, it was Sheriff Bud.

Henry was so excited by this inspiration that he threw a paper on the wrong porch and had to go back to get it. Of course she would listen to Sheriff Bud, but how could Henry get Sheriff Bud to tell Ramona to stop pestering him on his paper route? Write him a letter, that's what he would do. Sheriff Bud was always waving around handfuls of letters and wishing listeners happy birthdays and hoping they would get over the measles or something. He was always pretending he could see people in the television audience, too. Henry had never heard him tell a listener to stop pestering someone, but there was no reason why he couldn't. It would be worth trying anyway.

As soon as Henry finished his route he went home and turned on the television set. There was Sheriff Bud in his ten-gallon hat. This time he was wearing a false nose. He held a microphone in one hand, and between commercials was interviewing a row of children who had microphones hung around their necks. All the children said hello to many, many friends out in television land. Henry thought it was a silly program, although he still sometimes watched the cartoons that were shown between the endless commercials.

Ordinarily when Henry wrote a letter he used the typewriter, because it was more fun than pen and ink, but today he was in too much of a hurry to hunt around and poke all those keys. He found a piece of paper and a pen, and after his address and the date, began, "Dear Sherrif." That looked peculiar so he added another *f*. "Dear Sherriff" still looked peculiar so he consulted the dictionary.

Then Henry tore up his letter and started over. "Dear Sheriff Bud," he wrote in his best handwriting. "I need your help. There is this girl who pesters me on my paper route. She always watches your program so could you please tell her to stop pestering me? Her name is Ramona Geraldine Quimby. Thank you." Then he signed his name, addressed an envelope to Sheriff Bud in care of the television station, found a stamp, and went out to mail the letter.

As soon as the mailbox clanked shut, Henry knew his scheme would not work. Sheriff Bud received thousands of letters every week. He was always talking about the thousands of letters he received. He waved great handfuls of them around. Why would he pay any attention to one letter and a pretty smudgy one, at that?

But doubtful as he was, Henry somehow hung

on to a faint hope that Sheriff Bud might really read his letter and help him out. The letter would be delivered the next day but he might not have time to read it before the program went on the air. Maybe the day after . . .

Two days later Henry rang the Quimbys' doorbell about the time the Sheriff Bud program was starting. "Hello, Beezus," he said, when his friend opened the door. "I was wondering—how about a game of checkers before I start my route?"

Beezus looked surprised. She and Henry used to play checkers often, but since he had become a paper carrier and spent so much time working on the clubhouse, he had not found time to play with her. "Why . . . yes, come on in."

As Henry had expected, Ramona was sitting on a hassock in the living room watching Sheriff Bud, who today was wearing sideburns. While Beezus got out the checker set, Henry watched the program.

"And I want all you little folks out in T.V. land to do something for old Sheriff Bud," the Sheriff was saying. "I want you to tell Mother right now, *right this very minute,* to put Crispy Potato Chips, the potato chips positively guaranteed never to bend, on her shopping list. Yes, sirree, this *very minute.*" His smile filled the whole screen.

"Mother!" called Ramona. "Sheriff Bud says—"

"I don't care what Sheriff Bud says," answered Mrs. Quimby from the kitchen. She sounded very cross. "I can make out my grocery list without that man's help."

Beezus set up the checker board on the coffee table and, kneeling, she and Henry began to play. For once Ramona did not bother them, but Henry found it difficult to think about the game and try to follow Sheriff Bud at the same time. They both stopped playing whenever a cartoon came on, but Beezus had no trouble beating him twice in succession.

Once when the sheriff waved a sheaf of letters Henry's hopes rose, but Sheriff Bud only wished a lot of people happy birthday and told how many people had written in to say they liked Nutsies, the candy bar chockfull of energy. Henry wished he had said in his letter that both he and Ramona ate Nutsies all the time. And Crispy Potato Chips, too.

By the time the program had ended Beezus had defeated Henry a third time. Naturally Henry could not let this record stand. "I bet I can beat you tomorrow," he volunteered.

"I bet you can't," said Beezus, "but you can come over and try."

Henry left, and by working fast delivered all his papers on time. The next afternoon he once more presented himself at the Quimbys' front door, this time to show Beezus he really could beat her at checkers. He would forget all about Sheriff Bud. It had been silly of him to think his letter would be read out of all the thousands the television station received. Beezus had the checkers waiting on the coffee table and as usual Ramona was sitting on the hassock watching Sheriff Bud, who was wearing a pair of large false ears. His voice filled the living room.

"Ramona, turn that program down!" called Mrs. Quimby from the kitchen.

Ramona did not budge.

This time Henry was determined to ignore even the cartoons. Beezus made the first move with a red checker and Henry moved his black checker. Beezus jumped him, he jumped her, and the game was on.

"And now, kiddies out there in T.V. land, if Mother doesn't have a cupboard full of—" Sheriff Bud was saying.

Mrs. Quimby appeared in the living room. "Ramona, turn that thing off. I am sick and tired of listening to that man tell me what to buy."

"No!" screamed Ramona. "No! I don't want to turn it off."

"Then turn it *down*," said Mrs. Quimby, and went back into the kitchen. This time Ramona lowered the sound of the television set slightly.

"Your move," Beezus reminded Henry.

Henry studied the board. If he moved there, Beezus could jump him. If he moved there, he could jump her if she moved her man in the right direction.

"And now for today's mail," announced Sheriff Bud.

Henry could not help glancing at the television screen. Sheriff Bud was holding the usual handful of letters, but this time he was pointing straight ahead at someone in the television audience. "Ramona Geraldine Quimby, I see you out there," he said. "I see you out in T.V. land."

Henry and Beezus dropped their checkers. Mrs. Quimby stepped out of the kitchen. Ramona clasped her hands together and her eyes grew round. "He sees me," she said in awe.

"Ramona Geraldine Quimby," said Sheriff Bud, "I want you to do something that will make old Sheriff Bud very, very happy."

"Whatever it is, I'm not going to buy it." Mrs. Quimby sounded indignant.

Ramona leaned forward, her eyes wide, her mouth open.

Henry's eyes were just about as wide and his mouth was open, too.

Sheriff Bud sounded as if he and Ramona were alone. "Ramona, it will make old Sheriff Bud very, very happy if you stop pestering"—he stopped

and squinted at a letter in his hand—"Henry Huggins on his paper route. Do you promise?"

"Yes." Ramona barely whispered.

"Good," said Sheriff Bud. "We've got to get those papers delivered. If you stop pestering Henry on his route, you will make me just about as happy as it would if you told Mother you wanted Crispy Potato Chips for lunch every day. And now—"

But no one was listening to the television set.

"Henry!" shrieked Beezus. "Did you hear that?"

"I sure did." Henry was feeling a little awed himself. It had seemed as if Sheriff Bud really could see Ramona. He could not, of course, but . . .

"Honestly!" Mrs. Quimby snapped off the television set. "That man will do anything to squeeze in more commercials. Crispy Potato Chips! Really!"

Only Ramona was silent. She did not even object to her mother's turning off the television set.

She turned to Henry with her eyes wide with awe. "Do you really know Sheriff Bud?" she asked.

"Well . . . I guess you might say he is a friend of mine," said Henry and added, to himself, Now.

Then Mrs. Quimby spoke to her youngest daughter. "Ramona, have you been pestering Henry on his paper route again?"

Ramona looked as if she were about to cry. "I—I won't do it any more," she said.

"That's a good girl," said Mrs. Quimby. "Delivering papers is an important job and you mustn't get in Henry's way."

"I bet I know how Sheriff Bud knew about it," said Beezus with a smile. "Your move, Henry."

Henry grinned as he advanced his checker. Beezus promptly jumped and captured two of his men. Oh, well, what did he care? It was only a game. His paper route was real.

Henry grimaced at Ramona who smiled back almost shyly. Henry moved another checker, which Beezus captured. He did not care. His paper route was safe from Ramona. If she pestered him again, all he had to do was to say, "Remember Sheriff Bud," and his troubles would be over. It was as easy as that. He had finally hit upon a good idea that had nothing wrong with it. Not one single thing.

"I won!" Beezus was triumphant.

"I'll beat you in the next game," said Henry, and this time he was sure he would.

CHAPTER SEVEN

Henry's Little Shadow

AFTERWARDS Henry realized that he should have known something would go wrong with his plan to keep Ramona from pestering him. Now, because he was a friend of Sheriff Bud, Henry had become such a hero to Ramona that she wanted to follow him wherever he went. Next, Mrs. Quimby said that she was disgusted with the Sheriff Bud program and Ramona was not to watch it any more. Not ever. This left Ramona plenty of time for tagging after Henry.

The worst part of it was there was nothing Henry could do about Ramona's tagging along, because she behaved herself. She stood quietly on Mr. Capper's driveway while Henry folded his papers. Henry began to wish she would pester him so he could yell at her to go away. Fortunately, none of the other paper carriers thought much about her, because many small children in the neighborhood admired the big boys who delivered the papers. Henry was always glad to spring on his bicycle and ride away from her. If he had delivered his papers on foot she would have tagged after him.

Then one day at school Beezus said, "Henry, I don't think you are going to like what Ramona is going to get for Christmas."

"What is she getting?" asked Henry.

Beezus looked worried. "I'm not supposed to tell. I just thought I better warn you is all."

Henry did not know what to make of this message. He did not see how a doll or whatever it was that a girl in kindergarten was going to get for Christmas could bother him. As for himself, he hoped he would get a sleeping bag, because he had not saved his paper-route money as fast as he had expected. He had spent quite a bit on nails and a padlock for the clubhouse, and when he counted the money he had collected for his paper route he found he was short a couple of dollars and realized he must have made some mistakes in giving change. This cut into his profits, and after he had done his Christmas shopping he was still several dollars short of a sleeping bag.

Henry was not disappointed on Christmas morning when he opened a big package and found, not a sleeping bag, but a microscope. He could have a lot of fun with a microscope. It was so cold his mother would not let him sleep outdoors anyway, and next month he would have enough money to buy the sleeping bag.

It was not until Christmas afternoon, when Henry was folding his papers, that Henry found out what Beezus meant. He looked up and saw Ramona standing there on the driveway in her snow suit. Henry dropped the paper he was folding when he saw that over her shoulders she was wearing a cloth bag, a small copy of the one *Journal* carriers wore. It even had *READ THE*

JOURNAL embroidered on it in red yarn. Embroidered! It was terrible. In each half of her bag Ramona carried some old rolled-up newspapers. She also carried a battered Teddy bear in the front half. She was smiling proudly.

Naturally the other carriers practically laughed themselves sick at the sight of Henry's admirer. Red with embarrassment, Henry tried to pretend he did not see Ramona. He bent over and folded papers as fast as he could, so he could get out of there.

"Henry, see what Santa Claus brought me," said Ramona, ignoring the laughter. "Now I can be a paper boy like you."

The other boys whooped.

"Why don't you go home?" Henry asked crossly.

"I want to watch," said Ramona politely.

Henry could see that in spite of the boys' laughter Ramona was proud of her very own *Journal* bag, and there was nothing he could do about it, because she had kept her promise to Sheriff Bud and was being good. Henry could see that another of his good ideas had turned out wrong. Even when Ramona was good she was a problem.

Then Beezus, wearing a brand-new Christmas car coat with a hood, came hurrying up the driveway. "Come on home, Ramona," she said, then turned to Henry. "I tried to warn you. A *Journal* bag was the only thing she wanted for Christmas and so Mother had to make her one. She had a terrible time. She couldn't find a pattern."

Henry slung his bag of *Journals* over his shoulders. "Thanks anyway," he said ruefully, as he threw his leg over his bicycle and rode away from Ramona and the laughter of the other boys.

The next morning, when Henry woke up, he discovered that snow was beginning to fall, a few light flakes at first and then more and larger flakes. What luck! Snow during Christmas vacation. He looked out of his bedroom window and saw that there was already an inch of snow on the roof of the clubhouse. After breakfast Henry dragged his Flexible Flyer out of the basement to have it ready, in case there was enough snow for coasting.

All morning snow fell. By noon it was easy to roll up a snow man. The police blocked off a hill not far from Henry's house and all the boys and girls went coasting. Henry slid so much and got into so many snow fights he had to go home and put his clothes through his mother's clothes dryer before he could go out again.

Cars that did not have snow tires slipped on the icy pavement and skidded into the curbs. Some people who were fortunate enough to have their chains with them thump-thumped down the streets as the snow packed down into ice. By three o'clock Mr. Huggins came driving slowly up the street and skidded gently into a drift at the foot of the driveway. He said the stores downtown were closed and many people could not get across the bridges, because the streets were blocked by skidding cars. Mrs. Huggins looked into the refrigerator and the cupboards to see how much food she had on hand, because she could not go to market and there was no telling when the milkman could get through.

The whole city was in a wonderful state of confusion, and Henry enjoyed every minute of it. He hoped it would be days, even weeks, before the snow thawed. Then the mailman, a muffler tied over his ears and his hat on top of that, came puffing up the steps hours late. The sight of him reminded Henry that he too had work to do, and it was not going to be easy in this weather. Snow or no snow, the *Journal* had to be delivered.

Henry dried his woolen gloves in the dryer for the third time that day before he started out, this time on foot. At Mr. Capper's garage he had a long cold wait before the truck that brought the papers was able to get through. FOOT OF SNOW BLANKETS CITY was the headline that day.

In spite of the cold Ramona also waited in her snow suit with her little *Journal* bag over her shoulders. She kept busy by making a snowman on the driveway. "Fadatta, fadatta, fadatta," she said to herself as she worked. When the snowman was finished she tried her *Journal* bag on it. Henry hoped she would leave it there but she did not. She put it over her own shoulders again.

When Henry had managed to fold his papers with fingers numbed by the cold, he discovered that this time Ramona could tag after him, because he had to cover his route on foot. And follow him through the snow she did, about ten feet behind him, even though walking was not easy. In some places the snow had drifted, in others it was packed down into ice. Henry walked as fast as he could, but Ramona struggled along after him.

A man who was trying to shovel snow in front of his house grinned at Henry and said, "I see you have a little shadow."

Henry was mighty glad to see Beezus clumping through the snow in her boots. "Come on home, Ramona," she coaxed. "It's getting colder."

"No," said Ramona. "I want to go with Henry." She trudged along in her boots and there was nothing for Beezus to do but follow along and keep an eye on her.

Henry threw the first paper, which landed with a *plop* in the snow that had drifted on his customer's front steps. Softly a few flakes of snow fell on the paper. This isn't going to work, thought Henry. The papers would get buried on this side of the street, where the snow was drifting. Nobody would be able to find them. He struggled up the front walk, his heavy *Journal* bag banging against his legs, and picked the paper out of the drift. Then he rang the doorbell and handed the paper to his customer, who thanked him and said with a smile, "I see you have a little shadow."

"Yeah," said Henry, without enthusiasm.

Henry soon saw that it was too much work to wade through drifts with his *Journal* bag bumping against his legs. "Beezus, do me a favor, will you?" he asked. "Go get my sled for me."

"It will take quite a while if I have to take Ramona with me," said Beezus. "I could go faster without her."

Henry realized this was true. Ramona's legs were short and the snow was almost to the top of her boots. He did need that sled, though. "O.K., she can tag along with me," he said, knowing she would, whether he wanted her to or not.

Silently Ramona floundered along after him, and Henry grudgingly admitted to himself that she was not pestering him. She had a perfect right to be on the sidewalk, didn't she? If only she were not wearing that ridiculous *Journal* bag. And if only everyone he met would not say, "I see you have a little shadow."

Once Ramona said companionably, "There is an easy house number. One zero zero one." She was proud of her new ability to read numbers. Henry did not answer her.

It was not long until Beezus came, dragging Henry's sled behind her. He was mighty glad to lift the papers from his shoulders and set them on the sled.

"Come on, Ramona," coaxed Beezus. "You can be a paper boy some other day."

"No, I can't," said Ramona, in a small voice. "Henry always rides his bicycle, and I can't keep up with him." So on they trudged.

The next house on the snowdrift side of the street was the house of Mrs. Peabody. Henry took a paper from his sled, waded up to the front door and rang the doorbell.

"Why, it's Harry Higgins!" exclaimed Mrs. Peabody, opening the door just a crack so the cold would not come in. "My, but you are a thoughtful boy to bring the paper right to the front door!"

"His name isn't Harry Higgins!" Ramona shouted. "His name is Henry Huggins!"

Mrs. Peabody looked startled and opened the door a bit wider. "Is it really?" she asked Henry.

"Well . . . yes," admitted Henry, "but that's all right." Just the same he was grateful to Ramona for straightening Mrs. Peabody out. He felt almost kindly toward the little girl in spite of that terrible *Journal* bag.

"My, I am sorry," said Mrs. Peabody. "To think that I have been calling you Harry Higgins all this time when your name is really Henry Huggins. I don't see how I could have made such a mistake."

"Aw, I knew who you meant." Henry was embarrassed.

Ramona began to cry.

"Come on, let's go home," said Beezus impatiently.

Ramona cried harder. "I—I'm too t-tired," she sobbed.

"Why, the poor little thing," said Mrs. Peabody. "She's all worn out. If I could get my car out of the garage I would drive her home myself."

Henry looked at Ramona, standing there sobbing in the snow. Her face was red with cold and blotched with tears. With her boots buried in snow she looked even smaller than she really was. She rubbed her eyes with her cold, soggy mitten, and sniffed pitifully.

Henry's feelings were all mixed up. He remembered how she had locked him in the clubhouse and what a pest she had been. At the same time he was grateful to her, because she had told Mrs. Peabody his real name. Doggone it, thought Henry. Doggone it all anyway. Why did this have to go and happen? He felt sorry for Ramona—actually felt sorry for her. This was really the last straw. He did not want to feel sorry for Ramona in that stupid old *Journal* bag of hers. He tried hard not to feel sorry for her but he could not help himself.

"Come on, Ramona," he said, even though he didn't want to. "Get on the sled and I'll pull you home."

"I'll help," said Beezus gratefully. She lifted her little sister onto the sled in front of Henry's papers. "Now hang on."

Henry and Beezus took the rope and began to pull the sled. By this time the streets were almost empty of cars, and they could run, slipping and sliding, on the snow that had been packed down into ice.

Ramona stopped crying. "Mush!" she yelled between sniffs. "Mush!"

"Aw, keep quiet," said Henry rudely. He was in no mood to play sled dog for Ramona. He did not feel *that* sorry for her.

"Oh, thank you, Henry," said Beezus, when they had deposited Ramona on her front steps. "I don't know how I would ever have got her home without your help."

"That's O.K.," said Henry gruffly, and retraced his steps to start his route once more. And all because of Ramona. It seemed to Henry that he had never had a worse time delivering papers, not even when there was an extra-thick Sunday edition. Half his papers had to be delivered to the door or at least stuffed into the mailbox. He was too warm inside his car coat, but an icy wind began to blow through his trousers, chilling his legs. His boots were heavy and his gloves were wet again. He was tired, cross, and hungry. By the time Henry had delivered his last paper and dragged his sled home again, it was dark and snow was falling through patches of light cast by the street lamps.

"Henry, I was beginning to worry about you," said Mrs. Huggins, when he had stamped the snow off his boots and entered the kitchen.

"It takes longer to deliver papers in the snow," Mr. Huggins pointed out.

"It sure does, Dad," agreed Henry. "It sure does." And he thought, especially when someone like Ramona lives on the route.

The next day the snow had stopped and the sun shone on a sparkling world. The city began to recover. Snowplows cleared the main streets and by late afternoon most of Henry's neighbors had shoveled their walks. Henry was rested but so was Ramona. As soon as he started his paper route, there she was again wearing her little *Journal* bag. Henry wished all the snow was cleared away, so he could ride his bicycle again. Ramona, still very good, tagged along, and all the people who were now shoveling their driveways stopped working and smiled and said, "I see you have a little shadow." There was nothing Henry could do about it. A line of the poem he had once had to speak in school kept running through his head.

> "I have a little shadow that goes in and out with me,
> And what can be the use of him is more than I can see."

Boy, whoever wrote that poem knew what he was talking about!

The third day just enough snow had fallen to freeze on the cleared sidewalks and make them too slippery for Henry to ride his bicycle. Because delivering papers was still difficult Henry and the other boys gathered early to fold and count the papers. Henry was almost ready to start his route when Mr. Capper came around to check on the boys. He grinned at Henry. "Well, Henry," he said, "I see you got your name in the paper."

"Who, me?" asked Henry in surprise.

"Yes, Henry Huggins," said Mr. Capper, opening a paper. "Right here on the editorial page."

Henry could not understand what Mr. Capper was talking about. What would his name be doing on the editorial page or any place else in the paper? It must be some other Henry Huggins.

Mr. Capper began to read. "Dear Editor."

Henry understood that much. Someone had written a letter to the newspaper.

"Dear Editor," Mr. Capper read. "I wish to call attention to the fine work a boy named Henry Huggins is doing delivering the *Journal* in our neighborhood."

"Hey, that's me!" exclaimed Henry.

"I told you," said Mr. Capper, and continued reading for all the boys to hear. "Henry is always prompt and courteous, but it was yesterday during the heavy snow that I was particularly impressed with his work. Delivering papers that day was not easy, but Henry went out of his way to ring my doorbell and hand me my paper so that it would not get buried in a snowdrift. Not only that, he took time out from his route to give a little girl who was cold and tired a ride home on his sled. The *Journal* should be proud of this fine young citizen. Sincerely yours, Bessie Peabody."

At first Henry was speechless and then he felt as if he was suddenly growing about four inches taller.

All the other carriers looked at Henry with respect.

"Boy, I wish somebody would write a letter like that about me!" said Scooter.

"I've been delivering papers three years and nobody ever wrote a letter about me," said Joe.

"Me neither," said all the other boys.

"And Henry is our youngest carrier," Mr. Capper reminded them. He gave Henry a friendly slap on the shoulder. "Keep up the good work, Henry. I am proud of you."

Henry felt himself grow another inch. Mr. Capper was proud of him! He had said so in front of all the other boys.

On his way down the driveway Henry passed Ramona with her little *Journal* bag over her shoulders. She slipped on an icy spot and sat down hard. Before she could start to howl Henry boosted her to her feet, because he suddenly realized that if it weren't for Ramona, Mrs. Peabody would have written a letter to the *Journal* praising Harry Higgins, and Mr. Capper would have thought it was about a carrier in some other neighborhood.

Henry knew he had had a very close call. "Be

careful and don't fall again," he cautioned Ramona. "You might get hurt." Then he started delivering papers, with Ramona following ten feet behind him. Today this did not bother him. Mr. Capper was proud of him, so he did not care who tagged after him. Besides, he was too busy thinking what his father would say when he read Mrs. Peabody's letter in his evening paper.

Henry decided not to say anything to his father. He would let him discover the letter for himself. His father would be reading along and all of a sudden he would see Henry's name in the paper. He would probably be so surprised he would just about jump out of his chair. . . .

That evening it seemed to Henry that his father never would get around to reading the paper. First he dawdled over his dessert and asked for a second cup of coffee.

"Why are you so restless tonight?" Mr. Huggins asked Henry.

"Me? I'm not restless," said Henry, wishing his father would hurry up and drink that coffee.

"I'll carry your dishes into the kitchen, Dad," Henry offered.

Mr. Huggins looked surprised. He got up from the table and remarked, "Maybe I'll build a fire in the fireplace, it's such a cold night."

"That's funny, Dad," said Henry. "I was just thinking it was awfully warm in here."

Mr. Huggins turned on the television set.

That was too much for Henry. He couldn't wait any longer. "Say, Dad, did you read tonight's paper?" he asked.

"I glanced at the headlines. Why?"

"Well—I just wondered if you happened to read the editorial page," said Henry.

"Not yet." Mr. Huggins looked curiously at his son. "Why are you so interested?"

"I got my name in the paper." Henry could not keep the pride out of his voice.

"On the editorial page?" Mr. Huggins sounded disbelieving as he reached for the evening paper. He folded it back to the editorial page.

"There." Henry pointed at the letter.

"What is it?" asked Mrs. Huggins, coming in from the kitchen. She leaned over her husband's shoulder to read. "Why, Henry!" she exclaimed. "Wasn't that a nice thing for Mrs. Peabody to do for you!"

"Henry, I am proud of you!" said Mr. Huggins. "I don't care how much snow there is. I'm going right out and buy half a dozen papers so we can send copies of this to your relatives."

"Gee, thanks, Dad," said Henry modestly. He had waited a long time to hear his father say he was proud of him.

"I'll admit that when you took on the route and then got mixed up in building a clubhouse, I didn't think you could handle it, but you've done a good job," said Mr. Huggins.

Henry was pleased and at the same time a little embarrassed by this praise from his father.

Mr. Huggins went to the hall closet and put on his overcoat and hat. "By the way," he remarked, "how much more money do you need for that sleeping bag?"

"About five dollars," Henry admitted.

Mr. Huggins took out his wallet, opened it and handed Henry a five-dollar bill. "There you are. Tomorrow you go to the sporting-goods store and buy that sleeping bag."

"Thanks, Dad." Henry accepted the bill. "You mean I can sleep out in the clubhouse when there is snow?"

Mrs. Huggins spoke up. "You may not. Do you think I want you catching your death of cold?"

"But the sleeping bag is filled with down," Henry pointed out. "It's nice and warm."

"I don't care," said Mrs. Huggins. "You can't sleep out until we have some warm dry weather."

"O.K., Mom." Henry was agreeable, because he had not really expected his mother to let him sleep outdoors in the snow. He would have the sleeping bag and that was what counted. That, and knowing his father and Mr. Capper were proud of him and realized he could handle a paper route.

"Coming with me, Henry?" asked Mr. Huggins.

"Sure, Dad." Henry pulled his coat out of the closet. Good old Mrs. Peabody, he thought to himself as he put on his cap and pulled the ear flaps down over his ears. I knew she would be the best customer on my route. He picked up the paper to admire his name in print once more, and as he looked at it he could not help thinking, Good old Ramona.